This is My Exodus

Makenee Makeda

Trilogy Christian Publishers

TUSTIN, CA

Trilogy Christian Publishers
A Wholly Owned Subsidiary of Trinity Broadcasting Network
2442 Michelle Drive
Tustin, CA 92780

Rights Department, 2442 Michelle Drive, Tustin, CA 92780.

Trilogy Christian Publishing/TBN and colophon are trademarks of Trinity Broadcasting Network.

Cover design by: Jeff Summers

For information about special discounts for bulk purchases, please contact Trilogy Christian Publishing.

Trilogy Disclaimer: The views and content expressed in this book are those of the author and may not necessarily reflect the views and doctrine of Trilogy Christian Publishing or the Trinity Broadcasting Network.

Manufactured in the United States of America

10 9 8 7 6 5 4 3 2 1

Library of Congress Cataloging-in-Publication Data is available.

ISBN: 978-1-63769-484-8

E-ISBN: 978-1-63769-485-5

Contents

Contents

Dedication

I dedicate this book to my amazing children, Zydann and Akyliah. Let me begin by saying thank you for putting up with me as I transitioned into the woman and the mother God called me to be. To my first born, Zydann: from the minute you were born, you have been nothing but patient with me; you were born in a time when I didn't know who I was or whose I was; you've been with me through every season of my life, and I know it wasn't easy, but you believed in me, and you held on to the end. To my beautiful daughter, Akyliah: thank you for your hugs and kisses, and most importantly, thank you for always letting me know that I am the best mom in the world. My prayer for you both is that God continues to cover you under the blood of Jesus Christ and order your steps that you will only be led to His will for your lives; I love you both, and may our bond never be broken.

Foreword

"I met Makenee through a member of my church who is also from Jamaica. We were on the Daniel fast for twenty-one days, and she joined via our telephone conference line. I recall feeling her passion and love for Jesus Christ through the phone line. However, she was laden with pain from her past. She traveled to Savannah for the last day of the fast. After sharing her full testimony, by the unction of the Spirit, I told her, 'You must write your story.'

"This book is a result of her quest for freedom from the hurt and pain of abandonment and abuse. This work will resonate with many people who continue to carry scars from their past and have not been able to move forward in living the abundant life God promised His children.

"Prepare to experience every emotion as you read this riveting true testimony of God's intervention and a victorious turnaround in a life that seemed helpless and hopeless. 'This is My Exodus' will bring hope, courage, and strength to all who read it with a heart to receive."

—Pastor Lydia A. Rayner-Syed
Grace & Deliverance Kingdom Church of Christ, HUTL
Savannah, GA

Preface

From despondency to victory, from depression to being anointed, the grace of God has surely abounded towards me. I never, in a million years, thought that I would be an author, let alone an inspiration to my peers. I was abandoned by my mother at the age of two, and I never knew my father; I was sexually, physically, and mentally abused while trying to find solace in my existence. I struggled, trying to find my happy ending, and every glimmer of hope of such ending never sufficed, but this was it; for me, this was the last time I was willing to lose that which I desired, that which I knew belonged to me. I was determined to fight this time around; I refused to use God's unchanging hand to go further into the enemy's trap; I was tired of depending on people for my happiness and thinking that my sexuality was my identity. I knew that this person that was being presented to the world was not who I am, there was a greater within me that was screaming to get out, but fear prohibited me from making such a transition.

Fear of shame, guilt, and condemnation that I would have to face from others, but I was willing to risk it this time around, and by me saying yes to God's uncomfortable call on November 9, 2017, I experienced and encountered the one and only true God. Now, every day that the Lord graces me with, I will claim my victory in Christ Jesus and no longer be a slave to fear.

Introduction

This Is My Exodus is more than a story of trials and tribulations—it is a prophetic release from God. I never thought that my healing would manifest from me writing a book in a time when my life was in limbo, and my heart was broken from betrayal from the people I loved and trusted. As I stepped out in faith to lay myself bare before God and the millions of people who would be reading this book, known and unknown, my main purpose is to help shed light on the little girls and boys that are hidden within us. The unspeakable traumas that are wrapped so tightly around our souls that inhibit us from experiencing the goodness of God and the freedom that Jesus Christ suffered so selfishly to give us. Ultimately, the decision to be free is up to you, but I must confess the journey is not going to be easy, and there are going to be many moments when you feel like giving up and just work with what you've got. I would suggest that before you begin the healing process, go to Jesus in prayer because He sits at the right hand of God, interceding on your behalf, and ask Him to guide and lead you as you open the coffin that holds the stench of your defeat. And believe me, by doing so, whenever moments of despair arise and the spirit of fear rears its ugly head, your God will step in and lift a standard against the enemy who will be desperately trying to keep you in bondage. Deliverance is an ongoing process because we are born in sin and shaped in iniquity, but with God by our side, we can overcome each day by studying His word and always walking in love not only for ourselves but towards each other.

I hope my testimony will help you see that you were chosen for such a time as this and that your scars are not only yours but for others to be healed and set free. Therefore, are you willing to expose those scars and let the healing begin?

The Knock

I am in a place where I don't know how to move forward, I have been through so many obstacles in my life, and for the first time, I am stuck; it's as if I am in purgatory! I was on the right path, well, so I thought; I had everything I needed: I had a family that I always wanted. I was in nursing school, I was doing my Master's degree at the same time, and I had favor on my job. And then the rug got pulled from beneath me; my fiancé told me he was leaving me because he didn't love me anymore; we've been together for thirteen years, my son was his stepson, and we had a daughter together, she was eight at the time. Where do I begin, my life is a testimony, and as I am writing this, my heart is still heavy, and I am still having sleepless nights, like why I am here, I thought all that I have been through as a child, God would've at least deliver me from this thing I am going through. I don't even know what this thing is. All I know is that I am in it, and I don't know how to get out of it, so I am hoping that by the end of this book, I will be free because right now, it feels as if I am in bondage.

I remember the brown rug I slept on; they put me there because I peed the bed; not sure of my age, but I think I was about four years old. My mother left me with her best friend and migrated to the USA; I guess at that time, that was the best thing for Caribbean people; oh, did I mention I am Jamaican. Anyway, she left me there; at the time, I have three other siblings—one sister and two brothers, but they were placed with their grandmother, who is their father's mother. You see, from the moment I was born, I was born in adversity, my mom told me that the man who is my father refuses to accept me as his child, so here I am, motherless and fatherless, fighting to survive at four years old. I can still smell the Vaseline, and I can still see him coming into the room, where I slept on the rug; my mom's best friend had two daughters that I shared the room with: they slept on the bed, and I slept on the floor. He is the brother of my mother's best friend, I don't know his name, but I know he would come and get me, and he would molest me, and I could hear her sweeping outside; it's so haunting to me because every time he would come and get me, I could hear her sweeping outside. Anyway, this went on for years until my aunt came and rescued me.

My aunt—my savior—I tell you God always has a ram in the thicket! This was my aunt-in-law, my mother's brother was married to her, and like my mother, he left her with two children to pursue the "American dream," whatever that means. I remember she would come and get me on Sunday evenings and take me to buy ice cream with my cousins; I enjoyed that, oh, so much. I remember I would cry whenever she took me back to my reality, but even at that age, when I wasn't thinking or knowing about God, He was thinking about me.

This abuse went on for years, and then, finally, my aunt rescued me; not sure how this happened, but all I know I woke up one day, and I finally had my own bed to sleep in, but my journey was far from over, I would have to now encounter new devils as they say "new levels bring new devils." There is an unspoken pain that hovers over the homes in the Caribbean. If all my island folk would be honest about themselves, you'll be surprised to know how many of us struggle with being molested by a parent, sibling, or a friend of the family, but we were taught to never speak of these things; those words weren't said to us per se, but the expectation is to be a child and know your place. We show our love by putting food on the table and a roof over your head; there wasn't any affection showed; what is a hug, a kiss, and "I love you!"? Physical affection was not something that was shown in majority of Caribbean homes; you are child, and you must know your place that meant shut up, endure, and the best one is "our business is our business."

My new beginning, at least that's what I thought, my poor aunt—she took on something that she knew nothing about. Isn't it funny how we see what we want to see? God gives us a vision of doing great things, changing lives, but He never shows you the process of these visions; He only gives you the feeling of triumph. Now that I am older and have been through some things, I can now appreciate what my aunt did for me, how taking me in must have been a great decision and all the hate and lecture she got from doing so, and I can imagine every time I messed up the "I told you so" she got from family and friends. But when you're in God's hand and His perfect will, no man nor woman can interrupt His plan and purpose for your life.

> Before I formed thee in the belly I knew thee; and before thou camest forth out of the womb I sanctified thee, and I ordained thee a prophet unto the nations.
>
> Jeremiah 1:5 (KJV)

I knew that I was destined for something from an early age, it's not something that is explainable because it's a feeling that takes over your soul, even though my surroundings and situation suggest otherwise; there is an unexplainable being that's inside me that guides me, I now know that this unseen being is known as the Holy Spirit. I have been in many situations that I am supposed to be dead or imprisoned, but God kept that hedge around me when it was supposed to be kept, and He removes it when it was supposed to be removed. I can look back on my life as a child, and it makes me sad that no one noticed my pain and suffering, or maybe they didn't care because who was going to invest money in someone else's child. In the Caribbean, whenever a parent would leave a child behind with either a friend or a family member, the expectation was for that parent in America to send a vast amount of money because we were told that in America, the streets are paved with gold and life is a fairytale; what a misconception that plagued our people for years. I remembered someone suggested that my aunt should take me to see a psychiatrist because I was displaying disturbing behavior, and she replied, "I don't have any money for that." And who could blame her? She was doing the best she could. Remember, my mother was still alive, living the American dream with no cares in the world while my poor aunt was being tortured by me; well, the version that was crying out for help.

All I wanted as a child was to be loved; well, to be honest, what I really wanted was my mother; I cried to sleep many nights as a child, and I can remember one particular night, crying out to God to just let me see my mother one more time. I remember running home from school, hoping she would be there waiting on me or waiting around the corner, but she was never there. In fact, no one was ever there, so I started to develop coping mechanisms, and that's how I have been surviving throughout my whole life until now because all I ever wanted was to be understood and cared for emotionally, but instead, I was beaten down with cruel words, and insecurity placed inside me. You see, the enemy knows when you're destined for great things; that is why from a young age, he tries to destroy you, he uses people that are closest to you to destroy you, but as I said, God removes those hedges when necessary because in the end the Lord will be glorified! He will get His glory, and He promises to give you double for your shame.

Here, I am thirty-seven years old, wondering what happened to my happy ending that I was working so tirelessly towards, but how can I work on a happy ending without God? True happiness and joy come from God; it's only in Him we can find true peace and happiness. We were created to praise only Him, and the proof of that is no matter what we gain in this life, it only satisfies us for a time, but when we find true peace and happiness in God, it lasts forever! I finally realized that I was being pruned by God because I began to lose friends, I mean friends that have been there for me for the most part of my life, but there is a saying: whenever you find yourself in real trouble, you'll see who leaves and who's willing to stand with you till the end. Even the strongest of us have moments when the burdens of life seem too great. It's then that the Lord whispers to our hearts... "Come to me, all you who are weary and burdened, and I will give you rest" (Matthew 11:28, NIV).

High school was very hard for me; my emotions began to get the better of me. I was still living with my aunt, but it's like I wasn't living at all; I was lonely and desperate for love, so I met a man; yes, a man, a much older man. He showed me affection, and not experiencing any form of fatherly love, I got attached to him, and by the time you know it, I was pregnant not once but twice that both ended up being aborted. By this time, my aunt's brother came to live with us; here I go again, I would find myself in yet another situation where I would be a sex object. I often wonder why I was the one targeted and not my cousins, but as I grew older and began educating myself on my issues, I realize that child molesters usually prey on children who are normally neglected in some area of their life. I have met women that were sexually abused by their father while their mother was in the home, and even then, they were being neglected by their own mother.

My uncle was very nice to me: he gave me anything I needed, he would pick me up from dance class at nights, and even pay for it at times when my aunt couldn't afford to send me. So naive as a child, not knowing that he had his own agenda. I remember days when I didn't want to be the first one home from school; I would always make sure that there was someone home; my uncle didn't get the chance to molest me, but whenever he would see me alone, he would touch me where I was uncomfortable and whisper in my ear that he would pay me money to have sex with him. I will never forget my sixteenth birthday: he came up behind me and told me that he would pay me ten thousand dollars to have sex with me; my whole night was miserable, but I always knew how to suppress my feelings and keep it moving.

As I went through high school, living with my aunt was torture for both her and me. I was going through puberty, and everything else that was keeping me bound at that time was overwhelming. So, what do teenagers do at that age that felt alone and forsaken? Suicide! Yes, I tried killing myself, I took a whole bottle of pills that were prescribed for my uncle, and my uncle had kidney problems, so I took his pills. I was ready to die, but God had other plans for me. I vomited all night into the next morning, and no one knew what I did. I was so mad at God, Why would you allow me to live in so much pain and misery? But He kept silent, or was I too young to understand or even hear His voice? But even at that time, when I was too immature to hear His voice, I wasn't too immature to recognize His hands, holding back mercy and releasing grace in my life. I continued to live in misery, and when it wasn't my uncle trying to have sex with me, it was my aunts' boyfriend winking at me.

I was so afraid to tell anyone about what was going on; besides, who would believe me. People, oftentimes, disregard anyone that was alone, helpless, or less fortunate. People tend to find satisfaction within themselves whenever they find someone worst off than themselves. I kept on living and pretending that I was happy, and even me writing it now, I can feel my heart getting heavy; I think it's a feeling of shame and guilt that I am feeling. I feel ashamed because this shameful abuse happened to me, and I have to disclose it publicly and guilty because I feel as if I am betraying my aunt that did her best to take care of me despite the unfair treatment I had to face growing up in that house. I am very grateful for what my aunt did for me, and we still have a good relationship to an extent, but there is an underlying hatred she holds for me in her heart. Hatred is probably a harsh word to use because how can I think that she would hate me when she rescued me from my abusers? But I have a nagging feeling that I don't know the whole story as to why I ended up in my aunt's care. Besides, I was not received with love from any of her family members; they definitely hated me. One of my "cousins" that I was close to would say to me, "Why do you hang around them? They don't like you." And another one of my "aunts" would say, "Makenee, you should do good and let them see you." I know that they think that they were helping me by letting me know what was being discussed in my absence, but they didn't know that they were hurting me. I felt so ashamed whenever they would say these things to me, but I never let them know; I would just smile. But when I was alone, I would cry because I couldn't understand what I did that was so wrong that they hated me—a child that was abandoned.

Purpose in Pain

Some would say I ran away, but I was eighteen years of age, so I moved out. I just had to get out of there; I wanted to live my own life and do my own thing. After all, what could be worse than what I was going through at home, and who cares anyway; I was an orphan that wasn't going to amount to anything in life, so I left to live the life that was expected of me or was that the enemy in my ear. I remember thinking to myself when I ran away, That is why hasn't anyone come and find me. I guess my speculations were correct, they never wanted me around in the first place, and I wonder why my aunt would rescue me from the hellish situation to bring me into another. Maybe she didn't know what I was going through. She never asked what I encountered living there. I remembered one day I managed to see one of my aunt's close friends on the street, and she stopped me and said that she was happy for me and that I looked great, and when she heard that, I ran away; she was happy. This was one of my aunts' closest friends.

Why was she saying this to me? Was what I was going through visible to others? Was I not being a grateful person? They told everyone that I was. They wanted me to fail so badly, like Jonah waiting for Nineveh to crumble and die. I did fall at times, and they would rejoice, but God wouldn't let them rejoice for long! He would always part my Red Sea right in front of them. It was hard being on my own, but I was adamant about never returning back, there comes what may, and now here I am about to graduate from university with a Master's degree and a published author. The enemy knows the threat I would become in life, and he knew I would be giving my testimony, so he kept me bound by guilt, shame, and insecurity. *But God!*

I am in so much pain, but I am trying so hard to praise and worship through it because I know my pain has purpose, I know I am being pushed into my destiny, but it is so hard because I feel so alone, and even as I am writing this book, I must admit I am not sure if writing this book will set me free. I know only Jesus can set us free, and I am trusting Him every step of the way. July 1, 2019, is a day I will never forget. I was on my way to my last day of therapy, but I didn't know it was my last day, but God knew. Anyway, on my way there, I heard a voice say to me, "Makenee, you ask me for something and in order for me to give you what you ask for. I have to prepare you for it, so I had to take away the thing you love dearly to break your heart because your heart is going to be broken many times over where I am taking you and the children you are going to help." About twenty minutes into therapy, the therapist told me that I didn't need to see her anymore as far as she can tell my fiancé did me a favor, and sometimes other people have to make hard decisions for us. I began to think to myself, *Did she not hear about the abuse I suffered as a child and all the other unscrupulous things I went through?* But I agreed with her, and I left the same way I went in. Driving home, I began to ponder on what God has spoken to me earlier, and I was trying to figure out what it was that I had asked Him for because I had asked Him for so many things, and then it hit me like a ton of bricks. My desire was to open a children's home for abused children, and because I felt that at that particular moment in my life, I was doing good, I was ready to handle such a big task. Even though my intentions were good, I was not ready spiritually, nor was I ready mentally; I had a lot of work to do on myself. I never thought about the despondencies that would accompany my request. I thought I had been through enough travesties in my life to accomplish this task, but I was wrong. The family I worked so hard in attaining evaporated in one day, and I felt a pain I had never felt before because of the desires of my heart.

I am very grateful for what my aunt did for me, but most people would think that I am ungrateful because I made something of my life, and I owe it all to her! But I beg to differ, yes, she rescued me from a horrific situation, and I never went to bed hungry, and I always have clothes to wear and a warm bed to sleep in, but I had to pay for those things every day while I was living with my aunt. I never felt like I belonged at that house. And even today, it is very hard for me to visit whenever there is a gathering, and I am invited. I always make an excuse as to why I cannot attend. I know families have problems, but I think that they should work them out openly amongst themselves and address those issues and not brush them under the rug and pretend that they didn't happen; I, for one, feel very uncomfortable in deceptive situations.

I wasn't an easy child to handle or even love. To be brutally honest, looking back on my behavior as a child, it would have been hard to love me too. But I was a damaged child, I was sexually abused by two different men at age three, and that went on for some time. My mother and father abandoned me, so when my aunt rescued me, she had a lot to deal with. I remember feeling forced to be extra, or I was always trying to divert the attention from the poor orphan that aunty rescued. As an adult looking back, I can see where my aunt and colleagues made me feel less than, and even today, my aunt likes to point out my flaws to her children so that they can feel better about themselves.

I was about nine years old, and I remember being at church. And that particular Sunday, my Sunday school teacher asked me if I would like to stay for the adult service. He would often ask me to stay and sing—I guess he thought that I was a wonderful singer. Anyway, that service was different; it was like God came down and touched my soul, and I gave my life to the Lord that day. I was so excited, I ran home, and I told my aunt that I am Christian now. And I will never forget how she turned and looked at me with disgust and said in an angry voice, "You think that is how Christianity is; do you think you can be a Christian just like that?" The way she said it to me and the tone she used made me feel like I was unworthy to know God. And from that day, I lost interest in being a Christian or whatever I thought that was. I continued going to church, but I thought I wasn't worthy of becoming a child of God.

She never liked me at all from the day she met me. This was one of my aunt's sisters; she would say things to me like, "Why are you here? Nobody wants you here." And I didn't know if my aunt knew about it, or maybe she knew and just didn't care. I did not like this aunt at all, and whenever she would visit us, my stomach would be in knots until she left. She always looked at me with disgust, just me, though all my other cousins she liked, me she hated with a passion. I never knew why, and frankly, I don't think it would make a difference if I knew. The fact is she did not want me living with her sister, and she made me aware of that fact every opportunity she got. Looking back at those moments, I remember a little girl trying so hard to be liked and doing everything to stay out of her way so that I do not have to encounter those horrible looks and crude words. But I had to endure it because I did not have anyone to fight for me; I was all alone in this battle. If I could be honest, none of my aunt's sisters like me, no one to step in on my behalf. Now that I am older, I can understand the saying "hurt people hurt people" because when I look at their lives now, compared to the past, then they were working through their own struggles, and I was the perfect person for them to take their frustrations out on.

My mother was nowhere to be found in my struggles, I had no one to fight for me, so I had to fight for myself the best way I knew how. I lied, stole, and fought whatever I needed to make me feel worthy; I did that. My cousins never made it easy for me either, well, only one of them; I remember she would come home from school, and while she was using the toilet, she would let me tell her every detail about my molestation. Never knew why she did that, but I guess she knows. I never asked her why because she was older, and I was afraid of her, so I would tell her every detail of my rape. I remember I would make up stories about my life to others because I felt so ashamed that I didn't have parents, but I kept on going hoping one day my mother would rescue me or I would die. So, when I turned eighteen, I packed my bags and moved out; I was finally on my own. I can finally live the life I want to live, and most importantly, I didn't have to endure the stares of my aunt's friends looking at me with pity and disgust because some of them did, and I didn't have to spend another holiday with my aunt and her sisters and brothers.

It wasn't easy living on my own, but I was making my own decisions, and I didn't feel so heavy inside my heart, I didn't feel burdened, and I never woke up wondering what I did or what kind of trouble I was in. Even though it was hard, I was free physically but still bound emotionally, I still bore the scars of my abusers, but by that time, I had learned how to tuck it away and keep it moving, and that I did—I kept on moving. I had a couple of friends that I would hang with, and they, too, were from broken homes, and they were also seeking a way out of their troubles as well, so we were on a quest to become rich by being drug mules. Unfortunately, we happened to get entangled with some drug dealers, and I was the first to smuggle drugs to a foreign country. Looking back and even me writing this, I cringe; I cannot believe I did this. I would've never done such a thing at this point in my life, but I was desperate, and if I could be completely honest, maybe this was another suicide mission. I went right through without being caught, but let's stop here while I give God a praise break! Let me tell you about those hedges.

When God has a plan and a purpose for your life, it doesn't matter what the enemy throws at you, and whatever situation you find yourself in, when God has His hands on you, nothing can change that. I remember the plane ride; it was nerve-wracking, but I went through with it anyway; I would never forget when I got to immigration, the immigration officer came from behind the counter and walked me out to the front entrance. Now, I looked back on the situation that was God protecting me because He knew I was stupid and unsaved, but even when you're not thinking about God, He is thinking about you. When God has a plan for you, there is no devil in hell that is going to stop His plan for your life. Later, God revealed to me that the lady that walked me through the entrance was an angel. I know some might say, "Why would God do such a thing?" But when you are in God's plan, God will protect you when you are chosen to be used for His glory.

I became pregnant at the age of twenty-one; it was a horrible pregnancy because I was alone from the beginning; it was like I could not get a break on love or a normal life. Of course, your decisions always have consequences; he was always in the streets and had plenty of women. I finally found what I was looking for a drug dealer that was going to give me "everything." Little did I know, this, too, was another teachable moment in my life. Looking back on that relationship, I never knew what I wanted; I was just thinking I was going to have lots of money and living the fancy life, but that was just a thought, and it stayed a thought. He was good to me, he made sure my rent was paid, and I had food and money in my pocket, but he was never around. I have heard the saying, "Girls marry their fathers, and boys marry their mothers." Even though I never knew my father, I am beginning to think the spirit of abandonment was lingering in my life. I was told that when my family heard that I was pregnant, they rejoiced because they thought that this would be the end of me, or I would come, crawling, back to them, but I didn't. I don't enjoy holidays as much because tragedy always presents itself around that time of year. It was New Year's Eve 2001 when my world came crashing down; my son's dad was murdered in his apartment with a woman, who was then identified as his girlfriend. I was devastated because I was eight months pregnant, and I was not working and was about to give birth any day now. January 27, 2002, was the day I gave birth to my son, he was perfect, and I was determined to give him a good life, so I tucked away yet another unfortunate situation in my life and kept it moving. I kept on living, well, the outer shell of me, the survivor in me, at least, not the real me; so, I did what was necessary to put food on the table for my son and me, like being in relationships that were unhealthy for me, but I had to survive because I had no one but me, myself, and I.

When my son turned two years old, I migrated to the USA; it was like a dream come true. Even though I did not have a plan, I was just excited because this was where all my dreams were going to be established. The cliché that all dreams come true is true; I dreamt of living in America for as long as I could remember; I just knew this was where I belonged; this was the land of "milk and honey" for me; this was my Exodus! I remember the day I got my visa: I was so excited because it was very hard to get a visa in Jamaica without any kind of assets, family ties, or a job, and I went in there empty-handed and came out with a visa, this is where I shout, "Favor isn't fair." Unfortunately, this visa was only for one, so I was put in a position to leave my son behind! Sounds familiar, yes, generational curses do exist, but they can be broken when you use your experience as guidance. Don't get me wrong. I felt guilty leaving my son behind; I felt like my mother, but looking back, I now realize God wasn't only taking me on my journey; He was also taking me on my mother's journey. I got so much hate for doing this from my own family; they would say things like "she is just like her mother," "the same thing her mother did to her," "she's doing it to her son." They were highly upset that I got the opportunity to live a better life. They say that I would never make it and that I would be deported, they were predicting my future, but God was building it. I couldn't understand why they would want me to fail, I never did anything to them, and I had nothing; they had everything, but it was their hate that fueled my survival and my wanting to prove them wrong.

The night before I left my son, I cried the entire night. I slept with him in my arms, and I cried uncontrollably; even as I reflect on that moment, my eyes weld up with tears. The next morning, I drove to my best friend's house and said goodbye to him. He was crying; it was as if he knew I was leaving, it broke everything in me, but I knew I had to leave, but I also knew I would do whatever it takes for us to be together again. I knew he would be okay. I left him with my best friend and her family; we have been friends for over twenty-five years, and she was also his godmother. I was determined not to be like my mother, but at that moment, I had to be like my mother; I had to turn my back on my son—my own flesh and blood. I often say to people to be careful at the things they judge, scorn, or even pity because God will put you in that same situation to see how well you handle it, and I have proven this theory over and over again. So, now here I am, standing in the thing I judged my mother with for years; it was now my responsibility to start breaking those generational curses. God will always use one from among us to deliver a generation because, in Genesis, that was a promise He made to Eve that her seed will rise up and bruise the head of the serpent. We might not know which seed, but He is a covenant-keeping God, and whatever He says must be fulfilled.

The Journey

My mother, it sounds strange when I say the word mommy, mom, or mother because I feel like that name holds a lot of responsibilities for her pain and suffering along with all her children's. I have two brothers and two sisters, and we all share the same mother but different fathers. All my siblings know who their father is but for me. The man whom she says is my father denies it, and I ask him for a paternity test, but he refused. I think I've seen my mother about nine times throughout my entire life, and I don't think I have a general reaction of love and affection towards her. To be honest, it was mostly hate, resentment, and anger. I often wonder if that is the same reaction she has towards me, I have to realize that not because you have a child that does not make you a mother, nor does it make you a father. Is this an expectation that we place on people, or it depends on the situation? When my fiancé walked out on my children and me, I was devastated.

People around me told me that I must learn to love myself first because if I had love for myself, I wouldn't be so devastated when he left. But it was okay to feel hurt and pain because my mother abandoned me; I mean, in retrospect, she walked out on me too, so I wonder does love have boundaries or is it the cure that we all say is the answer? How could she have left me to go through all this turmoil? How come she didn't want me? Why didn't she love me? These are the emotions that consume me whenever I see or hear from my mother. Whenever I would hear my mother's voice, I would cringe; I think about all the things that I had endured in life and to think that your own mother caused this turmoil—well, this is what I thought before my encounter with God. My mother has a very strong personality, she is not an affectionate person, and I believe this is because she has been hurt throughout her life; she has never shared her story with me at this point in my life, but I can see the pain in her eyes, and you know what they say—"The eyes are the windows to the soul."

I arrived at JFK International Airport, I was so excited to be in America, but I was nervous about meeting my mother. She was supposed to pick me up from the airport, and I didn't know what to expect. I didn't know what the reunion would look like. I didn't know how I was going to receive her because it has been years since I saw my mother. As I stood there waiting for her,

I am thinking to myself, *Should I hug her when I see her? Is she going to hug me when she sees me? Or, Do I just wave at her?* For the first time in my life, I felt vulnerable. As I am writing, tears fill my eyes; this is supposed to be my mother, whom I haven't seen in years. I am her daughter; she carried me for nine months; we should have had an established bond, but here I am conjuring up ways on how to receive my own mother. I waited and waited, and no one showed up; she didn't show up at the airport. Can you believe that? Luckily, I had twenty dollars in my pocket, so I took a cab to my mother's house because I knew her address. She wasn't there when I arrived at her home, so I waited outside for her; thank God it wasn't winter.

My mother knew I was coming, and she didn't even mention to me that she would not be able to pick me up from the airport, but I guess she, too, was feeling the pressure of the reunion; well, that is what I am telling myself. Now that I have been through some things, I can see how terrified she must have been. This is worse than facing your fears in her defense; this must have been a nightmare, and I can see how not showing up at the airport gave her a little more time to get into character, and I say character because this was going to take someone other than herself to face this reality.

My mother has not seen me in over a decade, so you would think she would be happy to see me, but it was the opposite; she didn't even give me a hug when she saw me. It was just another day in the neighborhood for her; there was absolutely no excitement in her demeanor. She was as cold as ice. Her facial expression read, "Why are you here?" I was so disappointed and heartbroken; I was really expecting my mother to be extremely happy to see me; I thought that she would have flung her arms around me and told me how much she loved me and how sorry she was to have abandoned me and she is going to do whatever it takes for us to establish a bond of being mother and daughter. I thought that tears would be flowing down her cheeks, and I would be in her arms, sobbing, telling her how much I loved her, and I forgave her, but that wasn't the case because of her response to me. I responded back to her in the same callous manner.

Maybe, it was that simple for her; maybe, she had no regrets leaving her children. And should we blame her for that? After all, it's her life; she is allowed to make choices that are good for her. The only problem I have with this "movement" is that it affects others, and I am not necessarily speaking about me; I am referring to my aunt that had to support me while my mother was "living her truth," whatever that is. I think I reminded my mother of things she does not want to remember, or maybe that is just how she is. I was so uncomfortable being there in my mother's home, I did not know how to communicate with her, and I guess she did not know how to communicate with me either. She never asks about my son, her grandson, and she never asked what my life was like growing up without her; it was like I was her past that came back to haunt her.

Anyway, because I came to this country with nothing, my mother thought that she was going to have to take care of me. So, she called my sister in Florida and told her that I could not live with her because the landlord is going to raise her rent; that was what my sister told me. Can you believe that this woman really wanted nothing to do with me? But looking back, I can see where the hand of God was still moving in my life. I began to see that this wasn't her doing, but God's doing to put me in a position to accomplish His purpose for my life.

Florida, the minute I landed, I knew I was home. The weather was perfect, the streets were clean, and it reminded me of Jamaica, the weather that is. My sister was at the airport to get me; at least, she showed up, there she was my older sister, big sis, the person who was supposed to be there for me, to help you get on your feet in a new environment, but it was the opposite. My sister was battling demons of her own; she, too, was broken. Sometimes, we think that other people have it better than us because they have what we desire, but everyone struggles. My sister was looking for love and acceptance. Even though she had a relationship with her dad and she grew amongst her grandmother and her brother, life wasn't easy for her either. My sister came to live with my mother when she was a teenager because she tried to commit suicide, and so my mother came to Jamaica and took my sister only.

I always wondered why she only came for my sister, but when my sister told me what her life was like living with my mother, I realized my mother's only reason for bringing my sister to live with her was because she needed a nanny and a maid. She didn't really want to help her; she only wanted to help herself. It's hard to imagine or even think that your own mother has these feelings towards you, but society lets us think that because you gave birth to a child, love is inevitable. But as you go through life and experiences, you begin to realize that not everyone that has children is a mother or father. They can have you and not love you, and that does not make them bad people.

Living with my sister was not easy; her lifestyle was one that I could not adjust to. I was here on a mission; I had responsibilities, my son was depending on me. So, my focus was to get myself situated and create a home for him and me. I thought my sister would have understood that but I would soon come to realize I was on my own again, but this time I was around my immediate family, and still, I was being abandoned left to find my way. I lived with my sister for less than a year, and during that time, I observed her: she was somewhat like my mother, she lived for herself, and even though she did not abandon her son physically, she abandoned him emotionally. Both my mother and sister lived only for themselves; everything they did was for their own benefit. They never sacrificed anything, not even for their own children; they would always choose themselves.

My sister always partied; I guess this was how she numbed her pain, she and I had never really spoken about our childhood, but by just observing her behavior, I knew she, too, was suffering from mental and physical abuse. I started out babysitting because I didn't quite know how things work in Florida, and whenever I had a job opportunity, I would have to take my nephew with me. And his behavior was atrocious; she taught him not to respect me. Why—I do not know, but all I know is that I was burdened with taking care of my nephew, her child, and all she did was work and party. I was so unhappy and depressed I didn't know what to do because my sister did not want to help me in any way; my heart was also aching because I left my son, and I was missing him terribly.

As time passed, I began to find my bearings. I would work and save my money, and God made a way for me to obtain my green card. This, too, was another thing in my life that I had to fight for, but by this time, I had learned to accept my journey. But I knew that I was getting close to my destiny or the things I desired. Even though I wasn't fully emerged in my Christianity, I knew that I could always depend on God; there was a trust I had in Him, and I knew even in my darkest moments, He was with me always. I knew He was the only one that would never fail me, but contrary to this fact, later in my life, this very same belief that has gotten me through tough times would eventually be put to the test. God is so amazing; as I am writing about this chapter in my life and comparing it to where I am now, I can see how that moment was a preparation for this moment. Because of my immigration woes, I was introduced to the courts of heaven by the Holy Spirit, and that was where I gain knowledge on how to go before the courts of heavens when your prayer seems as if it is not being answered; yes, it will all work for my good.

The Grass Isn't Always Greener

He was so handsome; he literally took my breath away. The first moment I laid my eyes on him, I was in love or in lust, I don't know exactly what it was, but I knew I wanted to be a part of his life. We eventually became a couple, and it was great between us; we would spend a lot of time together. If I could be completely honest, this was the first relationship that I truly enjoyed. He was an excellent listener, and we both had a lot in common; he was the first person that I was with that I didn't want any kind of financial support from. Normally, if I am going to be in a relationship with anyone, I would always look for financial gain; I was never fully committed to them or the relationship; I was merely doing what I do best to survive. But it was different with him; we would talk for hours; he was the first person I opened up to about my past and all the horrible things I had suffered. He was very vocal about his past as well, and it was in those moments I soon realized we bore some of the same scars. I would love to tell you that my fight was over, but it was just beginning; but as I said, I was used to fighting, and I would give this everything I got.

He was the first to say, "I love you"; I have never heard that before from anyone, and I never said that to anyone that I have been in a relationship with, and if I did, I lied. But this "I love you" was sincere; I was really in love with this person, he wasn't perfect, and God knows I was far from perfection. I have been in a couple of relationships, but that's all; they were to me just relationships, I never valued them, and they never met Makenee. They have never met the vulnerably, kind, thoughtful, and loving Makenee; they only knew the bitter, unforgiving, vindictive Makenee. But when I met him, I was willing to let down my guard, I was willing to give up and tear down those walls and break those barriers, but there was a problem with this willingness of mine, and that is I didn't know how to tear down walls and break through those barriers because it was never shown to me and I was never in an environment that modeled such behavior, but I would give it a try because I loved him.

Be careful what you ask God for—He might just give it to you. I remember I opened up my mouth, saying, "I would like a pretty quiet thug." Go figure, you might not know what that means, but I know, and God knew what I meant, and I got exactly what I asked for, but when you're young and naive and not knowing who or whose you are, your decisions are based on your own understanding. I always wanted a family, I always wanted to belong to something or someone, and this was my moment, and this was my time to start my family. But what I didn't know is how to keep that family, and it took a lot of work to maintain a family, and I was lacking all sorts of skills in that area. But even in this chaotic phase in my life, God will still use it to His advantage to bring healing and deliverance to both my children and me.

As time progressed, we became inseparable; we would do every and anything together; I was in love. He was shy and funny, he would always make me laugh, and as I said, he was a good listener, and he never judged me or questioned anything about what I had disclosed to him about my past. He would always sympathize with me and shared something sacred about himself so that I would know that I wasn't alone and that he, too, has some scars. Like everything else that is worth anything to me, I had to fight to either get it or if I do get it, I had to fight to hold on to it. Yes, this relationship was going to be a fight like no other, and it was from both sides of the fence. His parents hated me because of the sins of my mother and my father. Why is it that I never had this problem with my other relationships? I got along quite well with their families, but the first time I ever wanted anything for myself, here comes the fight.

I was still living with my sister when we met, and he had just come from New York to live with his aunts in Florida. We spent a lot of time together; you know, the "honeymoon" stage of every relationship. I remember at nights, we would pray for each other, we would hold hands, and it was just an intimate moment; it was a spiritual moment for me as well because I've never met anyone like this, and I was almost sure he felt the same way. My first job was a babysitting job, and he would take me to that job every day and pick me up. And some days he would stay with me as well; he wasn't working at the time, but his parents were very supportive of him, but his aunts weren't; they would always speak down to him. He would confide in me whenever they would say hurtful things to him, and he would never tell his family because he did not want to spark a feud within the family. So, we would comfort each other the best way we knew how to, and I think those were the moments I held on to throughout our relationship because those moments were the moments that made me fall in love with him more and more.

We eventually moved in together; this was the first time I had ever lived with a man, and this was also the first time he had lived with a woman. It started out okay, he got a job working at a warehouse, and I was doing home health. I was so happy; I was finally beginning to see some normalcy in my life; I was finally going to have a family of my own. I would be able to decorate my own home, cook for my family, and have family dinners together; you know, everything that you see on television, everything that society says what a family should look like. But as usual, television and society do not show you the fights, the cheating, the name-calling, the sleepless nights, and the suicide attempts. Writing this is very hard, but I guess therapeutic at the same time because I never really spoke about this part of my life in depth, nor did I acknowledge that I was a victim and a victimizer of abuse. I know it seems implausible, but let me just say when you have been a victim for a long time, you adapt the ways of all your perpetrators, and you build a defense mechanism that eventually turns you, the victim, into the victimizer; and when you love something or someone, you think that victimizing them gains control because that was what was used to control you.

Punching holes in the wall was his favorite thing, and breaking the furniture—he enjoyed doing that too. Anything I loved or valued—he would break it, he didn't care, or should I say he wasn't aware of what he was doing? I say he wasn't aware because he was always drunk whenever he would go on these destructive rants. He was an alcoholic, and he did not become one; he was always an alcoholic; from the day I met him, he loved his liquor. I didn't know what an alcoholic was because I have never been around any, and as I said, this was the first man I had ever lived with. Before we lived together, he and I would drink together, and yes, he would drink a lot more than I did, but he was never abusive or angry when he drank around me. But I guess it was because we were not living together, and we have a saying in Jamaica "See me and live with me is two different things." And is not that the truth?

I often find myself wondering what I could've done differently back then, but God keeps reminding me that there wasn't anything I could have done; the script was already written for my life, and I was just going along with the script, I wasn't aware of the script because, in the book of Deuteronomy, He tells us that the secret things belong to Him, and because I was His secret, I was His. And this is one of the things that separates God from man. God knows the beginning from the end, I am the one that is new to my life, but God already walked through it; so, He knows exactly how this story would end. I know some may say that God would not have written such a script, but He wrote His only Son's script, and, in the end, God's will was done. And this is how I know my life is not my own because if I belonged to myself, I could have never made it this far, but because I belong to Him, I was able to endure. I was not surviving because of my own strength and capabilities; I was surviving because I was the moment He thought of me.

After living together for about a year and a half, my son finally came to live with us; I was so excited; noticed? I said—I, not we, was excited. To be honest, he wasn't mad about it, but he wasn't happy either, but I didn't care; I was going to do what I wanted to do because I had to be in control at all times. We never discussed having my son live with us. Even though he knew I had a son, but I never asked him how he felt about having a child in the home; he did not have any children at the time. So, I am sure it was scary for him, but as I said, I had a victim's mentality; I have to be in control. My son was six years old when he came to live with us, and immediately he fit right in; my fiancé was very nice to him, and he would try not to drink or curse around him, he would take him to McDonald's, cut his hair, play video games; he tried, and I tried to be the best mother I could as well. I wanted a family so bad that I was willing to do whatever it takes. Even though I knew we were not ready, but he was my son, and as soon as his filling came through, he was going to be with his mother because I know that I can trust him.

The grass isn't always greener on the other side; the reason I say this is because my fiancé came from a traditional family setting; his parents have been married for years, and that was one of the things I admired about his life. I thought that because he had both parents in his life to emulate, he would bring something to the table. I couldn't, but again expectations would yet rare their ugly head. Not that he didn't emulate his parents that he did to a "T," but it wasn't what I imagined a traditional family setting would be like. In fact, I felt sorry for him more than I did for myself because he had gone through so much and still was not able to trust his parents with his secret pain. How can you live with your parents and not feel comfortable around them? This was very strange to me, but as I said, I was learning, and in the end, those questions would be answered throughout my experiences as a parent. If you just keep on living, life will give you the answers you desperately seek, and those answers will not come from another's experience. If it is God who is ordering your steps, you will have gained those answers through personal experiences.

Grace

In 2009, we welcomed a baby girl; she was so beautiful; I was so happy and full of joy because I just knew that this was going to be our new beginning; after all, this was his first child. Those expectations again; why do I keep expecting him to fulfill my expectations? It was not until I began writing this book, God revealed to me that the reason most of my relationships failed was that I keep expecting people to live up to my expectations, and when they don't, I get disappointed. And that is how anger, bitterness, and unforgiveness creep in. I never realized that I was being so dependent on others to satisfy my desires. I enjoyed watching him being a father, he would bathe her, comb her hair, feed her, and he would take her everywhere. My son was happy that he was a big brother, and he would do everything for her; we were happy. We had Thanksgiving together, we had Christmas together, and I was loving it because even though my family was not perfect and it was broken in a lot of places, I was enjoying the fact that I had something that I always wanted, that was never afforded to me as a child, and that was a family to call my own. Christmas was the best we would wait. Until the kids were sleeping, we would wrap the gifts together, we bake cookies on Christmas Eve, and we would just enjoy each other. We tried to build a family of our own, but the foundation that we were trying to build on was not a steady one; in fact, there was not any foundation at all. We were just making it up as we go along, but the problem with that scenario is that, eventually, it would all come tumbling down.

His drinking became worse, and my attitude was intolerable; we were a hot mess. When my daughter was about three years old, I became extremely depressed; I would lay in bed all day until he came home from work. I remembered he would come home, bathe the baby and feed the kids and clean the house and then hit the bottle—I would just lay on the couch and cry all day. This went on for about six months; I was not working at the time because after I had my baby, I decided to stay home and go back to school. I eventually snapped out of it, pulled myself together, or I tucked it away like I normally do and created another world and started building on that one. This was a pattern that I developed throughout my life. I would have months of joyous moments, and then I would sabotage it with something from the past that he did or just anything stupid to start a fight. Back then, I did not know what I know now, but as I said, it will all play a part in not only my healing but the healing of others.

The year two thousand seventeen was one of the best and worst years of my life, but eventually, it would be a pivotal moment that I would never forget. This was when I knew what "when God comes knocking" meant, always heard it but never experienced it, and now He was at my door knocking. Everything was going great for my family and me, but mostly for me, I was beginning to see the light at the end of the tunnel. After everything I have been through throughout my life, I was like, Yes, God has shifted things in my favor. I thought that when God steps into your situation, that all things are roses and candy, but I was wrong. Everything I thought, I knew or imagined God to go right out the door, now I was going to be introduced to the man himself, and this introduction was going to be one I would never forget. Before I begin, let me just say that I was always a believer in God, I got baptized shortly after I had my daughter, and I was serving in the children's ministry at my church. I was ostracized by family and a few friends when I made this move. Some family members mocked me by calling me Sister Makenee, and they would say it in a sarcastic manner, but I held my head high and continued to declare the word of the Lord.

I graduated that year with a bachelor's degree in Supervision and Management with a concentration in Healthcare Management; I was elated. Can you imagine me graduating from college with a degree the least among them? That's what I thought because that was what was expected from me, a bag of nothing. But God, who is always watching and faithful, when God says, He will take you up when your mother and father forsake you, He means every word of it. He says that He watches over His word to perform it; how lucky we are to have a God that watches over His word that was planted in our lives to perform it or to bring it to fruition. I continued to stay focus because I thought the doors were finally opening for me, so I kept on knocking on those doors. I always had a desire to open a children's home for abused children, not just a building but a community, a real home. So, my educational path was always headed in that direction. I had accomplished getting one degree; now, I was on a mission to get others. As soon as I graduated, I applied for a position at a prestigious university for a place in their Healthcare law program, and I also applied for nursing school because I wanted to be well versed in what I was desiring, I didn't want to do it half-heartedly; I wanted to do it whole heartedly. So, I was willing to do whatever it takes to give back what God has given me.

I have always been a dreamer, meaning I often visualize what it is I want, then I go for it. Or should I say that measure of faith that was given to us? I utilize it at times, and I always use it in difficult situations. To be honest, I often take risks and then ask God to bless it because even though it might not be "lawful," I know God understands my intentions and motives, and I know as long as my motives are beyond my own personal gain, I know that God will give me grace; grace—the unmerited favor of God. I did it; I was accepted into the Shepard Law Master's program at Nova Southeastern University, and I was also accepted into the Bethesda College of Health Sciences. I was about to do the impossible; I wasn't sure, or should I say, I never knew anyone who was attending nursing school while doing their master's degree. But this is what I meant by me being uniformed; I was consistent in conduct. Nursing school was an associate degree, and it was also a private school, but it was very reasonable because it was owned by a hospital, the hospital that I was working at for a couple of years. However, I had a plan; I always had a plan because, as I said, my aunt made it very clear to me from early on, saying, "You do not have anyone to give you anything; so, you have to work harder than everyone else." I was hurt when she said that to me because, basically, what she was saying is that she is only going to do the bare minimum for me; the rest is up to me. Even though I was hurt by those words, it was those words that kept me going, and later on, God would shed light on those same words; or should I say He would give life to those words?

The school was going great for both of them. That is, I was doing the best that I could, and I was also working a full-time job and taking care of the household. I was still doing the cooking, cleaning, and laundry, but I enjoyed doing it. I just love being a mother and taking care of my household. I knew he appreciated it because he would tell me that he does. There were nights he would hold me when I would cry, and he would help with the dropping off and picking up with the kids in regards to school. I do not know if he was feeling insecure within himself because I was thriving, and he wasn't because he would make little remarks like, "Everything is working out for you; what about me?" But everything I was doing was for us, I wasn't oblivious to his incapability, and I was willing to do whatever it takes to maintain my family, even if it meant sabotaging my happiness and health for them. I just wanted to make him and my children happy, and I thought that if they could see how much I sacrificed for them...or should I rephrase and say: if he could see the sacrifices I am making for him, he would never leave me. I made a point to include my children because oftentimes, we use them as a crutch as to why we do the things that we do, but if we could be honest with ourselves, most of us that come from a background of abuse and neglect—we often put our needs first; not that we don't love our children, but longing to belong to someone or something will always be the driving force behind our existence until we become aware or it is made known to us, the victims of abandonment, then getting to worthy and self-acceptance are only words, spoken without transparency.

November 9, 2017, is a day that I will never forget. For a long time, I deemed it as the worst day of my life, but as I drew closer to God, it has become apparent to me that this day would soon give meaning to the scripture: "But as for you, you meant evil against me; but God meant it for good, in order to bring it about as it is this day, to save many people alive" (Genesis 50:20, NKJV). I have said this scripture so many times, and boy, have I used it out of context and misinterpreted its meaning, but I was about to embark on a journey with God Himself, who was going to teach and guide me throughout this next phase of my life. As I sat on the bed watching him throw his clothes in white garbage bags, I was so helpless because he had a determined look on his face; it seemed as if he was planning his getaway for some time. So I knew whatever I said or whatever I did was not going to change his mind. His attitude towards me changed as well; it was like he was trying to disassociate himself from me; he would treat me in the most horrific manner and say the most hurtful things to me. I asked him why he was leaving us, and he said that he was not happy anymore, and this having a family business was not working out for him; he wanted to be free.

It was a rainy night, and I remembered him sitting on the couch with our daughter, telling her that he will always love her and that they would spend every weekend together and that nothing would change between them. She was so in love with her dad and so innocent, she just said, "Okay, daddy." And they hugged, and he forced a tear or two, and then he left. He thought that he left with just his clothes, but he took almost everything away from me, and that meant that he also took from my children. This moment was one of the worst moments that I would never forget. Well, that's what I thought, but God was about to show me and teach me that with His spirit and teachings, I will be able to overcome, and not only will I be able to overcome, I am going to come out stronger, I am going to have power, and I was going to come out with more than what I went in with.

Grief is not something that we should ever ignore or take lightly; I have never met grief in this way before, it took my whole thinking. Everything I knew, everything I trusted in myself—grief stole that from me. I have been through some things in my life, but this was the first time I was literally brought to my knees. I was broken; I was on the verge of a nervous breakdown. I thought I was going to lose my mind. I could not eat, I could not sleep, and I couldn't even go to work. I became so depressed I had to apply for FMLA from work; I could not function at all. I eventually dropped out of nursing school, not by my own doing, because I was willing to continue. In fact, it was the only thing that kept me going, but God had other plans for me. So, he closed that door. God began to close all doors that would be a hindrance to His purpose being fulfilled in my life. Friends I knew for years that I personally gave my all too laughed and talked about me and eventually walked away. God was cleaning the house. At the time, I didn't know that it was God's doing; I felt that someone hexed me, or the devil was just out to kill me because everything around me was either collapsing or walking away.

I began drinking, smoking, clubbing, and being in relationships I had no business being in, but grief will do that to you. You start looking for comfort in the wrong places, but that scenario never lasts; especially, when it is God who is doing the reshaping and the inflicting. Yes, God does inflict pain because, without pain, you will never step into your purpose. That lifestyle became obsolete in a couple of months; then, I was left to face myself. During this time of "death," well, that is what I called it, I had to attend to my daughter and my son's broken heart. My daughter had always been a quiet, shy little girl in school; all her teachers would tell me it was such a pleasure to have her in their class. She would get awards for the best behavior. Every prize-giving suddenly became disruptive, and she was crying all the time. I remember the first email I got from her teacher, my heart broke because I knew she was hurting not only for herself, but she was also hurting for me because they would witness my constant breakdowns. As I mentioned earlier, grief took everything from me. My son began to act up in school; I could tell that he never wanted to be home because it was too painful for him to see me go through this, he was fifteen when this happened, and at that age, he was trying to figure out himself as well. So, this was really stressful for him.

I felt so alone; it is not like God stepped in right away and said, "Hey, it's me, God, that is doing this to you." No, I struggled with this for about a year and a half before I got any answers from God. During that time. My ex was so cold towards my children and me; he turned into someone that was unrecognizable even to his own child. Everything that he promised my daughter he would do—guess what? He didn't do it, and I remember I called him to tell him that our daughter was sad and needed him. He told me that I was her mother, and it was my job to comfort her. He did not give me any support whatsoever, he told me to put him on child support, and he was not going to give me any money until the judge gives him an order. One day, he sent my son a text, telling him how much he loved him and how it was a pleasure being his stepdad as if it was a job. He just resigned from, and then after that, he blocked our numbers. One day, my son came home and told me that he saw my ex on the road while he was out with his friends, and he said that he looked at him and turned his head. Can you believe that he turned his head? Not even a "Hello, how are you doing?" He had been in my son's life since he was six years old, the only father he knew. My son was practically his first child, and he just turned his head.

In My Own Strength

As I struggle to find myself and to put the pieces of my life back together, I now turned my anger towards God. I was so upset with God, and I had all right to be angry with Him because why He would take the one thing I wanted away from me. Why would He hurt me like this? I endured all that had happened to me as a child, and I never once blamed God. I never chose to be born in the situation I was in. So, clearly, it was chosen by God because He is the Creator, right? He knew me before I was formed in my mother's belly. So, clearly, He chose this life for me, so why would He take this one thing I wanted away from me? Up to this point in my life, I never complained. Instead, I was so grateful for where I was in my life and all that I had achieved, and I would testify to every and anyone how good God was to me, all the doors He opened for me despite my unfortunate background. I was livid with God; I said the worst things to Him; I blamed Him for everything that had ever gone wrong in my life, and I even called Him a liar. Yes, not one of my proudest moments, but I did. I even told Him that He was not real. I know it sounds horrible, but that is where I was; I did not care; I just wanted to die and to rid this heartache I was experiencing.

Thank God He is God and not like man because of the way I acted; I can honestly say I deserved some form of retribution. But like David tells us, "He does not treat us like our sins deserve, nor pay us back in full for our wrongs." Instead, He would love me even more. In fact, the worst I behaved, the more He would love me. Let me explain: my children and I were never hungry, my bills were always paid, they might not have been paid on time, but they were always paid. God provided during my time of grief and abandonment because it would soon become apparent to me exactly what He came for. I remembered one day I was throwing one of my tantrums, and he finally spoke; He said, "There she is, there is that little girl that I came for, that little girl that is trapped inside of you. That little girl that was never loved, that little girl that was abused and abandoned that is who I came for." And when God gives you revelation, it ministers to your spirit, it was like something on the inside moved within in me, and from that moment, school was in session.

I Love God!

I pondered on that statement for a couple of weeks, and even though I knew it was true, some truths are hard to face because facing the truth oftentimes means confronting the past, and going back oftentimes involves digging, and because I knew that everything that was buried did not get an autopsy, I was reluctant to pick up the shovel God was giving me. God is so patient with us; He knew what going back meant to me. So, He patiently waited for me to accept His unchanging hand. I tried everything not to go back to that horrible past of mine; I would try and manipulate God by threatening suicide, saying to Him, "You saved my life just to put me through this torment." I was referring to when I tried committing suicide as a teenager; can you even fathom me trying to manipulate God, and as God would actually be moved by it. To be honest, manipulation was one of my strongest suits; I have used my abandonment story on many occasions to gain favors in a few situations. I even used it on God too, and it worked, at least that is what I thought until I found out about grace!

The crying and self-loathing tapered, I was finally getting some relief, but my journey would be far from over. You see, God was in control of this mission, so every emotion felt, whether it being happiness, sadness, or anger, the thermostat of my life was only controlled by God during this season of my life. He was preparing me for something bigger than myself, and I have taken it as far as I could, and now it was time for Him to take it to where He wants it to be. But in order for him to do that, my spiritual being would now have to line up with what He had declared when He was singing over me.

> For whom he did foreknow, he also did pre-destinate to be conformed to the image of his Son, that he might be the firstborn among many brethren. Moreover, whom he did pre-destinate, them he also called: and whom he called, them he also justified: and whom he justified, them he also glorified.
>
> Romans 8:29-30 (KJV)

Killing the flesh, a term often used by preachers, but what does it really entails, notice I did not say what does it mean because we know what it means, but it is the process of killing the flesh; that is what should be taught in church. With killing the flesh, we gain free-dom because it is within our fleshly desires; the enemy has kept us in bondage because we seek the things of this world instead of seeking the things of God. So when it's time to take back that which was given to us through the shed blood of Jesus Christ, the enemy is going to do whatever it takes to keep us from discovering what true freedom in Christ really means. I was not as verse as most people where the Bible was concerned, I knew a few scriptures that I have learned from Sunday school, and that was as much I honestly knew. I always thought that the only people that God spoke to were preachers or prophets, and only through them would God reveal His plans for us. But I was wrong. If you were like me, thinking that God only speaks through prophets and preachers, let me tell you that God speaks to everyone, and you do not need a prophet to tell you your future or what God is saying about you because God will give you the answers you need if you seek Him.

I began working again; I took the night shift because I was having trouble sleeping, so the night shift was perfect, and it was only three nights per week. It was one of the best jobs I ever had, I had the luxury of working on the maternity ward, and I enjoyed every bit of it. It was a pleasant distraction for me, but that is all it was: a distraction from what God has spoken to me about the little girl trapped inside me. If I could be completely honest, I think it was embarrassment that was keeping me from venturing down that path of recovery; I think I was so ashamed of that little girl, I was ashamed of her because she was damaged goods, and I was embarrassed that it was me. It was not a little girl that was another person; that little girl was me. For so long, I had disassociated myself from her; I did not want to accept that those things had happened to me. I didn't want to accept that my mother abandoned my father and me disowned me; I did not want to be in that group of people. So, whenever I would talk about my past or testify about it, I spoke about that little girl, but I never truly accepted her.

Seven months into the job, God told me to quit; I did not complain because even though I was loving the experience, I just wanted to stay home in bed and cry all day and night. I wrote my resignation letter that same night and emailed it to my director, and two weeks later, I was home. Little did I know that God was about to literally show up in my life. And for these next couple of months, I would be on a personal revival with the lover of my soul and the lifter of my head. I began going to church faithfully because I thought that my inconsistency in attending church was the reason God was punishing me, so I started going back to church; I started paying my tithe and even gave sacrificial offerings on occasions. Let me step outside of this moment and give insight into that moment.

Going back to church was not my desire; it was God's desire. I did not know that at the time, but as He began to teach me, He begins to reveal. Even though He was preparing me for my purpose and reshaping my character, He did not want me to be anointed without vision, and not vision for my purpose but a heedful vision. Be-

fore my "suffering" began, I had never really delved into
the things of the church or the people, for that matter.
On Sundays, I would take out the "church me" and pres-
ent her to the congregation. But not this time; I was in
trouble, and I needed help, so I went there, not knowing that I was not the only one who had a Sunday per-
sona. But that's not the point I am trying to make here.
As I mentioned earlier, God was building my character,
and in order to do so, sometimes, He will use people to
reflect that which we display so that we can see who we
are, not to condemn us because there is no condemnation in Christ but to give us an opportunity to become
the sons and daughters He called us to be.

If the church doors were open seven days a week,
I would've been there. Even though I wasn't clubbing,
smoking, or drinking anymore, I was still looking for a
way to rid my pain, but I was still grasping at the wrong
things. I know you're thinking that church would be
the best choice for such a devastating time, and it is for
some people. Church is where the sick should go; this is
where healing and deliverance take place; so, why am
I not being delivered? Why is there no relief for me? I
went to the altar every week for prayer, anointing oil
plastered on my forehead, speak in tongues, ran all over
the church; I shouted and screamed but nothing. I went
to church sick and went back home sick, and it is not
that I was not calling on the name of Jesus some nights;

that's all I could say is just Jesus! But what do you do when God Himself is the one who is inflicting the pain? How do you pray that way? How do a "baby Christian" like me handle the God of the universe?

I recall on this particular day, February 26, 2018, let me just say this: I was journaling during my time of "death," so that is the reason I can give dates whenever there was an encounter with God. Anyway, the situation got so heavy for my daughter; she was crying uncontrollably on this day, and nothing I said or did could have comforted her; she missed her dad. My daughter was extremely close with him; they practically did everything together; he took her to school in the mornings and picked her up occasionally from school; they had a special bond, not even I could get in on it. But it was okay, I admired that because I knew firsthand what it felt like not to have a father, so when I saw how God had blessed me in terms of turning it around for my daughter, I was extremely grateful. I remembered going into the bathroom and closing the door, I fell on my knees, and I cried out to God and said, "God, help me please; speak to me, Lord, speak to me, I am begging you." I was desperate, and it wasn't a cute cry; it was a gut-wrenching cry, and to my surprise, he did. This was the first time I had an encounter with God, and I'm sure. As I'm writing this book, I heard His voice gently saying, "Malachi 4 verse 6." I was not an avid reader of the Bible back then, so I did not know what Malachi 4 verse 6 was saying. I knew the book of Malachi, but I never read it, so I got off my knees, open my Bible, and turn to the book of Malachi. Let me just say at this moment as I am reflecting, what a mighty God we serve! "And he shall turn the heart of the fathers to the children, and the heart of the children to their fathers, lest I come and smite the earth with a curse" (Malachi 4:6, KJV).

As a child, I was always singled out or compared to everyone and not in a good way. I remembered this one moment, to be honest, I never forgot it, but anyway, I had just started high school when I got my first report card, and it was better than my cousins', and my aunt, with a disgusted look on her face, turned to me and said, "You really make Makenee report card better than yours." And I don't think it was as much as what she said. Even though those words were harsh, I think it was the disgusted look on her face that is engraved in my mind. It was a look of disgust and "How dare you think you can do better than my child?" I think that was the day I stopped believing I could achieve anything. I started doubting myself as far as school was concerned, so I started rebelling, and I stopped caring about my education. I was held back once in high school and eventually got expelled for academic and behavioral issues. But even then, God was pulling the strings, so I am no longer upset with my aunt because she, too, was being manipulated by the puppeteer.

As time passed, I began to get stronger, but the stronger I got, it's like the weaker I became. One minute I would be up, believing God, fasting, and praying, and then the next minute, I will be down and crying and wanting to give up. And I did this for quite some time; I fasted, and I prayed because I felt that if I fasted and if I prayed, God will restore my family, but it didn't happen. It wasn't about the restoration of my family, it was about the restoration of the little girl that was hidden inside a big woman, trying to handle life, trying to be more than what they said that she would be, but in order for her to become what God had ordained for her, she had to deal with the little girl that was never dealt with. When my fiancé walked out, I saw someone that I never knew existed; even my friends were looking at me funny; they were like, "Who is this person?" "Where is this strong Makenee that I know ?" "Who is this weak person?" To be honest, I did not even recognize myself.

Let me shed some light on the God that loves us. Everything He does to us is for us; every pain, every disappointment is going to work for our good but for His glory. God waited patiently for me to stop throwing those tantrums, and then we had an encounter. It was October 18, 2019, when the glory of God fell upon me while I was in devotion. You see, the night before

I prayed a prayer to God, I was finally letting it go; it is what I had in mind for my life. I guess I was so used to fighting for everything that I did not realize that this was not a fight I would have to face alone. I didn't recognize that I wasn't alone in the fire. I wonder how many good things have come my way, and I did not recognize them because I accepted a lie from the enemy. When you have adjusted to your circumstance and accepted the hand you were dealt, anything that presents itself outside of that norm is not comprehended. But when it is God who is fighting for you, victory is inevitable, and you will know if it's God who's fighting the battle because, unlike family and friends, He will never walk away from the fight, not until the battle is won.

God took me back to a day when I was lying on the bed at my in-law's house, and I was listening to a Hillsong CD ("Shout to the Lord"). The song was "I love you so much," that was my favorite song on that CD, and I will just worship that one song for hours and hours and hours, but God took me back to a particular day, He even showed me what I was wearing, and He said to me, "You were not a Christian, you didn't even know who I really was at the time you've heard of Me, but you didn't know Me. You were in a broken place, you had lost your son's father when you were eight months; pregnant, you were homeless, you had no money, you had no family, and you heard that song, and you worshipped me not because you wanted anything from Me, but you were grateful for what you still had left, and that touched my heart." He went on to tell me that He misses that moment because I never worshipped Him like that ever again, and He was right. I was not ungrateful; in fact, I was always grateful for every opportunity and every door that God was opening for me, but the thing that changed was my motive. I started worshipping Him for the things that He was doing in my life and not for who He is; it became something for something kind of relationship. That experience broke my heart, not because I felt condemned my heart was broken for God; it was like at that moment, God showed me His heart and how He waited for me to come back to Him.

The Grave Side

"The secret things belong to the LORD our God: but those things which are revealed belong to us and to our children for ever, that we may do all the words of this law" (Deuteronomy 29:29, KJV).

From that moment, God began to reveal Himself to me. He began to give me the mysteries of the Bible and the mysteries of Himself. He was not a friend; He began to reveal Himself to me as a Father. God began to share with me the why's of my life, meaning why I had to go through all the things I went through and how He was in control the entire time. My Father began to deal with the little girl in stages, and He also began to reveal Himself to me in stages, believe it or not, the first conversation He and I had, or should I say the first mystery He revealed to me was the scripture that says, "Then said Jesus unto his disciples, 'If any man would come after me, let him deny himself and take up his cross and follow me'" (Mathew 16:24, KJV). God began to reveal to me that Jesus's cross did not begin when they literally gave Him the cross; He revealed to me that His cross began the minute He was conceived. He began to explain to me that Him being conceived by the Holy Spirit was in itself a controversy and travesty; He said even though we were taught that Mary was chosen by God, that doesn't mean that she wasn't human and had some resentment. And He also spoke about Joseph and him being a man having to explain to his friends and family that his unwed wife got pregnant by the Holy Spirit. He told me that in order for Jesus to be the kinsman-redeemer, He had to be kin to all our circumstances, and that is why He can be touched by our infirmities because He knows what it was like to be unwanted from birth.

This revelation was relevant to me, and God will only reveal to you in stages and what pertains to you and also what He is preparing you for; He told me that He gave me this revelation first because He wanted me to know He knows why my life began the way it did, and He is in complete control of the outcome. He wanted me to know that even Jesus, His only begotten Son, faced adversity from the moment He was conceived, so I need not be dismayed because I was also chosen to carry a cross that would one day bring freedom to His people that have been in shackles and bound by the enemies lies. You see, oftentimes, we blame the enemy for our mishaps, but sometimes those unfortunate situations are ordained by God so that in the end, His people will be set free and His name be glorified. The scripture tells us, "And I, If I be lifted up from the earth, will draw all men unto me" (John 12:32, KJV). He told me that in order for Him to be lifted up from the earth, He has to be seen as a spiritual being, so His miracles that He performs are beyond human comprehension, and by that, He's lifted up by man; with praise and by doing so, He draws us to Him because He dwells in our praises.

My Father pointed at the shovel and said, "Let the digging begin." Of course, the first "body" I had to dig up was my mother's, and it was a body I wanted to stay buried because why should I be the one to examine my mother's body. It's not like I single-handedly buried her, she literally placed herself in the grave, and all I did was shovel the dirt on top of her, but He wasn't having that. As much as how my behavior or even my actions towards this situation were justifiable, my Father would not at the least accept my reasons as to why I could not forgive my mother. What was so intriguing to His approach was that He didn't bring up my past, He didn't badger me with things that I had done, that He had forgiven me for, the only thing He said to me was to call my mother and tell her I forgive her.

I remembered that day clearly. I called my mother, and I began to speak to her in a way she never expected. I never once disrespected my mother or anything like that, but my conversations with her were normally empty, but this time I was compassionate; it was like I was trying to woo her into accepting my forgiveness. I started out by telling her that her leaving me wasn't her doing—God had ordained it the minute I was conceived; I went on to tell her that God was doing wonderful work in my life and that I forgave her and I loved her. My mother, in turn, said something to me that I would never forget, and I kid you not. For an entire week, I was in tears, and my heart was truly broken; she said, "Thank you, but I just don't know how to forgive myself." Even now, as I am writing, tears fill my eyes. For years, I held a grudge in my heart for my mother, not knowing that she was hurting too, and my mother was not only hurting because she left me, but my mother also left all four of her children; can you imagine the burden and heartache she faces every day? My perspective changed from that day, not that I still didn't need answers, but I began to understand that the victimizer's hurt is more severe than that of the victims.

God teaches through your mistakes, or should I say He teaches through your misinterpretations because a lot of times, we interpret things wrong, and it's not like we do these things intentionally. Sometimes, things we do are intentional, and even then, it's done out of anger and hurt, but when God has you in training, don't assume anything or add anything to His teachings because of trust and belief; God does not need an interpreter. As I begin to embark on this newfound journey with my mother, I was so excited, I was like I am going to teach my mother everything that God has been teaching me, and I truly wanted to get my mother to a place of rest and inner piece especially when she began to open up to me about her childhood and all the things she had to face with her mother. I began to get the answers that I needed, but I must admit it wasn't easy, but as I said, we, or should I say I, misinterpreted what God said to me; remember, the only thing God said to me was to forgive my mother, but now I wanted to save her as if I was Jesus.

My mother and I would talk almost every day, and I would minister to her and send her scriptures and just encourage her, but it wasn't easy because my mother is a very prideful person, so you know I had to be very patient and thread lightly whenever I was ministering to her because getting to a place of healing requires digging, and not everyone wants to dig. I mean, if it wasn't for God coming down off His throne literally for me, those bodies would still be buried, including hers, so I had to show the same grace and mercy that God had shown to me to her, and it was extremely difficult. I began to realize that I wasn't the only one who had justifiable answers for my detestable behavior; my mother had her own justifiable answers as well. And for the life of me, I couldn't understand how she convinced herself that abandoning her children was okay, but God was only showing me that not because abandoning my children wasn't my "thing," we all have a "thing" that we justifiably bury.

God will sometimes create a situation in your life to teach you a thing or two; therefore, do not be too hard on yourself when the walls come tumbling down. It was Valentine's day of 2019, and my mother sent me a text message asking that I called her when I got home from work because she wanted my opinion on a matter; I was like, no problem. I was excited because I was like; finally, she's meditating on the scriptures, and she has given some thought to our discussions on how to get to a place of healing, so I was excited about our upcoming conversation because I was sure we had a breakthrough. I was wrong; my mother wanted to do one of her abandoning acts again on my sick brother, and I wasn't having it. I was so angry at her suggestion; she wanted to put my brother in a nursing home because she did not want the responsibility of being his caregiver. And I was thinking to myself, Why she can't see that God was giving her a second chance to make it right, to do the right thing for once? And then it hit me. Her admitting that she cannot care for my brother is not her abandoning him or her leaving us in Jamaica as children were her way of doing the right thing.

I know it sounds crazy because how can a mother leave her own children, but as my mother ranted and raved on the other end of the phone, I began to well God began to reveal to me that my mother was as human as they come, I began to reflect on our previous conversations and what she had told me about her upbringing and how her mother left her and her siblings for another man. And it was at that moment I realized that my mother was only emulating what she had been taught, but it was still unsettling to me because I was placed in that same situation, and I chose not to make the same mistakes my mother made. I fought hard for my children not to endure the pain and suffering I did as a child. So how is it she did not feel the same way about us? What was holding her back to love us and want us? And then God whispered to me, saying, "Is not that she doesn't love you? She is afraid to love you because the first person she ever loved turned her back on her, so she was afraid to love because she did not want to endure that pain again."

That revelation had me thinking beyond my own reasoning capabilities; God began to explain to me that husbands and wives, boyfriends or girlfriends are not the only ones that create insecurities. The majority of the time, insecurities are developed from childhood, and because we are so young to comprehend it, we oftentimes blame it on our first failed relationship when, in fact, our insecurities stem from the ones we first give our hearts to, that is our mother or our father, and once that love is mishandled, we, the mangled, become protective of what is left of our ability to love and believe it or not, some of us are left with nothing. And at that moment, God revealed to me that my mother was one of the ones that were left with nothing, and only He, Jehovah Rapha, the God who heals, will be the only one to bring love back into her heart because He first loved us.

I was really overwhelmed with this revelation from God because for so long, I have held on to hatred in my heart for my mother; it was like I held her captive in my mind and in my heart. She was the one I would blame whenever things went wrong in my life, and in retrospect, how was I wrong. If she hadn't abandoned me and did what she was supposed to do as a mother, my life would be much different. But I was wrong; God wanted me to know that the mother who abandoned me then would be the same mother she is now, hurt and broken. I wouldn't have gotten the support I needed because whether she was there in my life or not in my life, the person she is now is the person she would've been then. So, even though it seems as if I was abandoned and, yes, I was, it was good for me because my aunt had more to offer than she, my mother, did. I didn't want to hear those words from God because, from my experience with my own children, children don't care about the circumstances that surround their mother or father; as long as they are with their parents, they don't care where they're at or what they eat, they just want to be with their parents. But that isn't true; we tend to think the grass is greener on the other side. As I began to speak to my friends that I grew up with in Jamaica and become transparent with them about my situation, they began to be transparent with me.

My eyes began to see, I mean really see, that we are truly not our own; I had a friend that was being molested by her own father, and her mother was living in the house and a prominent churchgoer. When I found this out, I was shocked because I have envied her for a long time because she had what I wanted—a family. Another friend of mine disclosed to me that her dad was gay while being married to her mother, and they had to live with this as a family, and I did not know this. As a child, and we all grew together in the same community, we played together, went to church together, and I thought I was the only one that was living in shame, not knowing that they, too, were envying the fact that I didn't have a family, they wanted what I had, and I wanted what they have. The Bible tells us to be content in whatever state we are in, and I am beginning to understand what that means. God knows what is good for us, even if it hurts, and believe me, it hurts, but this is one thing I tell myself if I am praying about it and God does not give it to me, that means that it is not good for me, and I trust Him with my life.

Trusting God with your life is pretty hard; wait, let me rephrase that statement: trusting God in times of despair and uncertainty is very difficult, especially when it was not expected. As I walk through this valley of death, I began to realize that once God steps into your situation, there is absolutely nothing you can do to speed up the process or, for that matter, bring forth this miracle that He promised. When God steps into your situation, the only thing you can do is be still and know that He is God, and that is all you can do. You cannot praise your way through it like we are taught in church, and I know this may raise some eyebrows among the religious community, but that's just how it is. God revealed to me that not every situation He's responsible for, but He will deliver us from all situations, but the ones He permits, he does not need our input, meaning we can't pray, dance, fast, or manipulate our way out of it. And an example of manipulation is a sacrificial offering, and trust me, I know I did a few sacrificial offerings myself, and I still came up short in regards to this breakthrough I was so desperately seeking.

I was still being processed by God even though I thought that I was over the biggest hurdle of my life, which was forgiving my mother; I thought that I was "cured" and ready to walk into my purpose, but little did

I know that was just the tip of the iceberg because now that I have removed the dirt from the coffin, it was time to expose what was buried inside. And once that lid is lifted, the stench of bitterness, insecurity, abandonment, manipulation, shame, and self-loathing would be anxiously waiting to be autopsied. I had no choice this time but to finally face the inevitable because by now, God had revealed enough of Himself to me in letting me know that He was not giving up on me. And at that moment, the scripture that says, "Being confident of this very thing, that he which hath begun a good work in you will perform it until the day of Jesus Christ" (Philippians 1:6, KJV) ministered to my spirit. This is one of the reasons I enjoyed writing this book because as I write, He reveals Himself, and, yes, He absolutely reveals Himself through His Word, I have heard this scripture many times, but now, that He has placed physicality to His word, it just shows me how intentional our God is.

Removing the Lid

God is such a gentleman, or maybe, in this case, I should refer to Him as amiable; He gently wooed me into my healing. I finally gained the courage to remove the lid, and it was a night that I will never forget. It was Halloween night, and my daughter's father had texted her asking if she's going trick or treating, and for some reason, I became so angry, and my heart boiled with hatred. I thought I had forgiven him and that I was finally in a safe place, meaning if I heard his voice or even saw his face, I wouldn't feel such rage, but I did what I always do with my hurt and pain, I buried it, and I forgot I was being processed by God; so everything that was buried was going to be exposed and dealt with. I went into my closet and wept for hours; I called on the name of Jesus; I wanted to be free from the bondage of bitterness because that was exactly what it was. I was extremely bitter towards him because of what he had done to my children and me; I felt like a woman scorned and used and tossed aside like garbage. I had to call out his name and everything he had ever done to me and release it to God. When I emerged from the closet, I felt a little better, but I knew that was just the beginning of this body.

Bitterness—one of the hardest multilayered emotions to accept; this emotion is mixed with anger, disappointment, and fear, so it's easy to justify bitterness because in order to become bitter, simply means that we were victimized. In addition, instead of dealing with the offense when it happens, we allow the offenses to seep into the inner parts of our souls, and every so often, we retaliate by being vindictive to the person that hurt us, not realizing that bitterness hid as revenge, and then revenge justifies after all I am just doing to you, what you already did to me. With the help of the Holy Spirit, I began to see myself; I began to really deal with the issues that I thought were never an issue in my life. I thought that I was truly an overcomer because I have risen above the naysayers, but God was teaching me that rising above negativity and negative people is not about worldly possessions or achievements.

Therefore, to truly deal with bitterness, we have to ask ourselves who has suffered at the hands of our revenge in the past or who are we being vindictive to now in our lives. Once you can honestly answer that question, then letting go of the bitterness becomes easy, I am going to save you the trouble of letting you think that it's on you to do this, but it is not. I know this might sound cliché to some people, but Jesus is our burden bearer; that's why He died on the cross. So letting go simply means repenting, which means asking for forgiveness and then giving it to God. It is not going to be easy because, remember, we have an accuser of the brethren that consistently accuses us, meaning he brings up our past, making us feel guilt and shame, so we become weak, and we feel as if God has not forgiven us. Forgiveness is not a feeling; it is a free gift from God; remember the cross I spoke about earlier; yes, Jesus paid the price for all our corrupted indiscretions, and all we have to do is accept what is freely given to us.

As I reflect on bitterness and on how the enemy, the accuser of the brethren, convinced me that being revengeful was acceptable, I can now compare it to what the Holy Spirit has taught me. You see, sometimes, God will let the enemy have his way so that when he steps in to show us a much better way, there is a comparison between what is right and what is wrong because it was through my bitterness I lost the ones I loved, but now that the Holy Spirit, who is our teacher, taught me that bitterness simply derives from unforgiveness and hides as revenge, I am no longer in bondage with the spirit of bitterness. The Bible tells us, "For we do not wrestle with flesh and blood, but against principalities, against powers [bitterness], against the rulers of the darkness of this world, against spiritual wickedness in high places" (Ephesians 6:12, KJV) (brackets added for clarity). So, yes, bitterness is a spirit to all who are wondering why I gave it a label.

As I reveled in not only ridding myself of bitterness but actually getting a one on one with the Holy Spirit on the break-down of the what and the whys of bitterness, it was time to face the stench of *insecurity. Insecurity* is uncertainty about oneself and a lack of confidence. Who knew that I was in bondage of this spirit? I always thought that I was a confident person. If you should ever ask anyone that knows me, they would be in utter disbelief that Makenee was insecure. They would say things like, "She is always well-dressed, her hair is always neat [Jamaican jargon], and she has accomplished so much." And even I can attest to such praise because, truthfully, I really believe I was a confident person until my fiancé walked out on my children and me. I began to question my worth; I actually told myself that I was worth nothing and it was my fault why he left; I had never felt so low in my life. I never thought that I would be looking in the mirror and criticizing myself.

God will allow you to hit rock bottom because that is where He does his building, so He allowed me to beat myself up so bad that I contemplated suicide again. I thought that I had failed my children; you see, everything I was doing was for my children. I didn't want them to live the life I had lived, of not having both parents in their lives, so I would've done anything to keep our family together even if the foundation was unsteady. Oftentimes, hurt mothers or fathers would either vow not to put their children through what they went through or they would emulate that which they have gone through, but the truth is the outcome is pretty much the same. I say this because the Holy Spirit revealed to me that not because we did not abandon them physically, but we abandon them emotionally. I was trying to build a family on rebellion, not on love or in Christ-like I should; I was rebelling against my mother and father for abandoning me. Being rebellious means resisting authority or control, and trust me, I was doing just that to my fiancé and my children.

I always wanted to be in control of my house, and because I knew my fiancé's weaknesses, I played on them, and don't get me wrong, He played on mine as well. I am not in any way, shape, or form justifying him leaving, but this is my book, and this is my story, so I am telling my truth. I knew that he dropped out of school very early in his life, so I took advantage of that, I was well-educated, coming from Jamaica because my aunt made sure of that, so I would help him do little things like filling out job applications or anything that seem difficult to him but easy for me. I wasn't taking advantage in the sense of not wanting him to achieve, but I thought that if he saw how intelligent I was, he would consider me to be an asset in his life, believe it or not, that is a sign of insecurity. I thought that I had to be better than him in order for him to stay with me; I never thought that Makenee was good enough for him, but who was Makenee really at that time? Did I really know who I was or even accepted me for me? So, picture two: insecure people trying to raise a family. "Delight thyself also in the Lord: and he shall give thee the desires of thine heart" (Psalm 37:4, KJV).

Oftentimes, we believe that God answers our prayers only when we pray to ask for something, but I got news for you, we have a God that not only hears our prayers, but He sees our hearts' desires. I used to desire that my fiancé would stop drinking and serve God, my heart genuinely desired a family, and even though it wasn't perfect, I always told God thanks for saving my life and giving me this wonderful family, and did you know that was exactly what He was doing? Everything that I am going through now is just a preparation for what is to come, but it is not as easy because the whole process requires faith, not in the process but in God. Normally, when God is doing great work in your life, the first and the only thing He will give you is a covenant, this is His word, and normally, it comes from the Bible, and He will always confirm His word. And once that process is over, then it is up to you to receive it, and receiving this covenant requires *faith*.

Still trying to grapple with the reality that I didn't think I was good enough was very hard to accept, but I know that it was no turning back, I couldn't pretend anymore, and my Father would not allow it. But the question was how I know that I am enough. Is it a feeling? I know to some people this is unfathomable, but believe me, it is not. As I pondered on my truth that I didn't think I was enough, the Holy Spirit began to reveal to me that accepting oneself is a choice and being insecure does not stem from one area in our lives; oftentimes, when we fail in the area that we placed emphasis on, we tend to believe that it's because we did not have what it takes, and that is the reason we fail. But it's our failures that actually tell us that we are enough; it is in our failures that we regain our strength and gain new wisdom. I delve deeper into this revelation, or should I say I was still being taught by the Holy Spirit. He revealed to me that if you have ever overcome anything in your life, this is a definite indication that tells you that you are *enough*.

Abandonment. How does one place physicality to this word? I don't believe anyone that has ever been abandoned can give a clear definition. This spirit is a spirit, in my opinion, the foundation for all other spirits; I believe this is the place where my trauma or maybe your trauma developed. My trauma started developing when I was first molested at the age of three, and the reason this happened to me was that I was abandoned by my mother and my father. Therefore, being abandoned opened the door to me being bitter and feeling insecure. I have dealt with the spirit of bitterness and insecurity with the help of the Holy Spirit, of course, but now it was time to pulverize the foundation of abandonment, and once this foundation is completely obliterated, then I can start rebuilding a foundation that will open the door to contentment, warmth, sweetness, and confidence, to name a few. But before the pulverizing begins, I have now grown custom to the Holy Spirit, my helper, revealing and healing as I close the door on abandonment.

Firstly, let me just say being abandoned is never your fault; I never knew this because my mother's action towards me was very aloof. I remember when I was a little girl, I would call my mother almost every day, collect from Jamaica, just to hear her voice or to share a bit of closeness with her, but instead of her explaining to me that it was very expensive for her, she changed her number. That crushed my soul, another instance of feeling, or should I say being abandoned, and I am sure that that situation opened the door to spirits of its kind, anyway, as I began to drill into this foundation, the Holy Spirit revealed to me that oftentimes when people abandon their children or any situation that seems insurmountable, it's not the victims that they are hiding from; it is actually themselves.

I was confused at this revelation because why would I, a child, put so much weight onto my mother? Why did she feel the need to hide from herself because of me? I began to question God, "What about me that made her cringe and become so withdrawn that even the sound of my voice brought her discomfort?" And He answered, saying, "Because you are the little girl she used to be, and dealing with you means dealing with her the little girl that she has never accepted." I understood exactly what God was telling me. Even though my mother has never told me about any physical abuse that she had endured in her life, apart from the verbal abuse that she suffered at the hands of her mother, I am sure this kind of hurt is generational. Again, my heart broke for my mother and my siblings as well because here I am experiencing these moments with God, getting the answers I need to start rebuilding my life, and they were still reeling from the pain of their past and now living in the pain of my mother's abandonment.

I could feel my spirit returning to my body, and my soul is renewed. For so long, I yearned to be free, but I sought the things of the world for freedom whilst ignoring the one whose true freedom originates. As I painfully endure the stench of my coffin, I must admit that the smell was fading, and every now and then, I would get a whiff of victory, so I pursued him. I knew it was God who was drawing me; I knew He was the one adjusting the air in my thermostat, and let me just say, whenever He would give me a whiff, it was breathtaking. I was addicted to the smell, and I wanted it to linger always, so I chased it, and in chasing it, I was chasing Him.

Manipulation. This is where the victim manipulates friends, family, and people in an unscrupulous manner. This was another spirit that had me in bondage, and I knew I had to be honest about every area of my life during this process; there were times when I would use my sad story to gain favors from people, especially people who were close to me and knew my story well whatever part I chose to tell them. And in doing so, they would, in turn, give me whatever it was I was seeking; I never thought that what I was doing was wrong because I did have a sad story; I was, in fact, a motherless and fatherless child. But as you know, God searches the deep things of our hearts not for His pleasure but for our healing, and my Father wanted me healed, so He brought this spirit to my attention.

The Holy Spirit began to show me that using the unfortunate things that had happened to me to gain favor was me giving it a place in my life; it was like I was making it my identity. I was beginning to believe that without it, I had nothing else to offer; you see, whatever we magnify, we glorify, and without realizing that, this presumptuous spirit that was hidden as "gaining favor," I used it to fuel my desires. Let me explain. Without knowing this truth about being manipulative, the Holy Spirit revealed it to me in a more dissected composition. I now understand that my desire to build a children's home was not only me being kin to it and wanting to save many lives; it was also based on me being manipulative. Even though I was attaining the degrees that were required to accomplish this desire of mine, it was only fueled by the fact that I was abandoned and abused; I knew that once I told my story of being abused and abandoned, I would receive pity I needed from whomever; I needed to gain such notoriety.

My intentions were absolutely genuine, and God saw that. But the application was disingenuous, and He wanted to give me the desires of my heart; God saw that I was struggling morally, so He stepped in to perfect that which concerns me. I was kin to the abuse, but I wasn't kin to the healing, and I didn't have anyone around me to shed light on the path of healing. And it wasn't that they were bad for me, but it was because the healing I needed could only come from the one true healer, who is Jesus Christ. Who else knows our pain and sufferings? The Bible tells us that He humbled Himself so that He could be touched by our infirmities. Humbling himself means that He was willing to be kicked and beaten, among other cruel acts, just so that I would be able to experience true healing. So, to finally put this body known as manipulation to rest, I can now forgive myself for being manipulative to others, and yes, I had to apologize to a few people that I had manipulated to "gain favor," and believe me, it felt great another spirit being placed under subjection.

"For your shame ye shall have double; and for confusion they shall rejoice in their portion: therefore in their land they shall possess the double: everlasting joy shall be unto them" (Isaiah 61:7, KJV).

Shame. A feeling of humiliation or distress; I struggled with this spirit for a very long time. In fact, this was the first emotion I experienced as a child. I was so ashamed of who I was because of the abuse I had suffered at the hands of men and the abandonment of my parents. Even at an early age, I knew what shame was; it was an emptiness in my soul that no matter what I did, the depth of this turmoil could not be filled. But what was I trying to fill it with? As I reminisced on my childhood into adulthood, I realized that unbeknownst to me, I was trying to fill something which I now know to be my soul. How does one fill their soul when you never even had the chance to experience the things that were taken from it? I never had the opportunity to experience real joy, love, and most importantly, inner peace, so in retrospect, how can I fill something I knew nothing about? And that was what has led me to this point in my life.

As I began to analyze the things that were taken from me, I asked God, "How do I recover all, and how do I rid myself of the spirit of shame?" He replied saying, "You have to first remove the I because, without Me, you can do nothing." That still small voice gets me every time because, with those simple words I received in my spirit, I began to realize that I was doing it in my own strength and understanding. I felt that I had to heal my wounds, forgetting that He tells us in Psalm 27:10 (KJV), "When my father and my mother forsake me, then the Lord will take me up." This scripture reads differently when you actually get into a place of complete surrender, and the only thing you can do is to let God have His way, and that was exactly what I was determined to do. I was trying for so long to fix what others have done to me, not knowing that God was there waiting patiently to give me beauty for ashes, and with that being said, I surrender all!

Reminiscing on how far I have come with my healing, I am extremely confident that by the end of my book, I will be walking in complete freedom as was promised by God. In the book of Hebrews, God promises us a divine rest, and this can only come from resting in His Son, Jesus Christ. I must admit I never understood what it meant to rest in Christ; I have always heard Christians or even pastors say, "That if God gives you a word, you should believe and rest in the word He gave you." God told me that He was going to restore my family, so I rested in what He told me. Well, at least, I tried to, but for some reason, I just could not find rest until I finally asked God how do I rest in what He had told me. You see, it's not that I didn't believe that God isn't capable of doing what He has promised; my problem was when it was going to come to pass. Therefore, whenever I didn't see it coming to pass, my heart would become sick. Until finally, I asked the right question; it is always important to ask God the right questions, not assuming anything.

The Holy Spirit began to reveal to me that resting in the promise should never be the focus; resting in Jesus, the one who is capable of bringing the promise to pass, should always be where my hope lies. Sounds wonderful but not easy because I am not just going to forget about the promise, but I was determined to draw closer to Christ so instead of pretending that I can do this on my own. My prayer from that night on was for Jesus to teach me how to rest in Him. The word is what teaches us how to rest in Jesus Christ; the Bible tells us that "Thou wilt keep him in perfect peace, whose mind is stayed on thee: because he trusteth in thee" (Isaiah 26:3, KJV). The operative word there is trust; without trusting that He will keep us in perfect peace, if our minds stay on Him, then we will not find the rest that we desire. Therefore, trusting in His word should give us the confidence we need to find divine rest.

Finally, the last body self-loathing, also known as self-hatred; oftentimes, when we hear this word, we quickly associate it with the physical aspects of our being, but I have come to learn that this theory is absolutely untrue. I struggled with this spirit because not only was I sexually abused, I was verbally abused as well, but I buried those hurtful words in the stench of self-loathing. Growing up, I was criticized a lot, especially about my thick thighs, but that wasn't what I buried, the things that we normally bury are the things that hurt us the most, and the reason we bury them is that oftentimes, the ones that hurt us are normally intimidating, so we become fearful to confront our abusers. Before I get into the what and the whys of the verbal abuse that caused me to self-loathe, let me just say this culture plays a lot in what is considered to be verbal abuse.

In my culture, verbal abuse is not perceived as abuse, I'm thinking because they are just words, and where I am from, if you are not physically wounded, then what are you complaining about? And to be honest, I have never heard anyone that I grew up with speak about verbal abuse; I think that because we are such proud people, we do not admit that we have been verbally abused by a spouse or a parent because of doing so, we are portraying weakness. Anyway, growing up, I was constantly told by an aunt that I wasn't wanted and what I was doing there, meaning why I am living with her sister. It was a Sunday morning, and I was getting dressed for church. I believe I was about ten years old, and I remember I was so sad and broken. Basically, I was missing my mother even though she never showed any interest in me, but I was hoping that she would one day come and rescue me. I remembered I was crying uncontrollably, and my aunt began to yell at me, saying, "Where's your shoe?" And I, in return, said to her, "My mother didn't buy me any." And I think I said that to her just for sympathy or to gain some kind of comfort. My aunt looked at me in such disgust and yelled out, "Your mother doesn't love you."

I was so ashamed when she said that to me because my cousins were there, and they just stared at me angrily; I could tell that they were also getting annoyed with me. I never knew why my aunt said that to me; she never spoke about that day, and I never said anything to anyone; I just suffered in silence. I guess that was the day I became promiscuous, angry, and rebellious, I didn't care what people thought about me anymore, and I hated who I was. The only thing I wished for every day was death, but it never came, even when I tried taking my own life. So here I am, faced with the spirit of self-loathing, determined to put it to rest by not leaning on my own understanding but with the help of the Holy Spirit, my teacher.

I often wondered why the victims must be the ones that suffer, why is it that some of us never get the opportunity to rise from the ashes. I began thinking about children that commit suicide because they had no hope; men and women who suffer from addiction because they never healed that little boy or girl that they tucked away, and most importantly, the little boys and girls that are currently being abused by someone they trust. The Holy Spirit began to reveal to me that there is always healing whether in life or in death, but there is always healing, and of course, I had to ask, "Why isn't there healing for everyone here on earth?" Because to me, in saying that, there is also healing in heaven seems like an answer that cannot be challenged. Why did I survive and not others? Why am I getting this one-on-one healing from God, Himself? What I am trying to say is that why was I chosen; what was so special about me that He chose me?

God began to reveal to me that as I begin to walk in my purpose, I will begin to see the reason I was chosen; He went on to say that people who are chosen normally bring redemption to other people's lives by laying down their own. My spirit leaped at this revelation, and immediately my soul rested; it rested because my understanding was enlightened, and I no longer feel unworthy of this call. If you are at the point where you cannot find any worth within yourself, if you continue to struggle with self-loathing, give it to Jesus because only He knows exactly what you're facing. Hebrews 4:15 (KJV) tells us, "For we have not an high priest which cannot be touched with the feeling of our infirmities; but was in all points tempted like as we are, yet without sin." Have confidence in those words, I do because my friends walked away, family members laughed and reveled in my despair, but God stayed with me; He held my hand and restored my life. Not my physical life because to restore something, you have to take what was broken and make it new, my soul was what was broken, my spirit was low, but God came into my life and restored my soul and lifted my spirit, and with boldness and confidence I can say that it is well with my soul.

The Test

The process of becoming who God anointed me to be continued on a daily basis, I would love to tell you that I woke up one morning, and my heart was all new again, but I soon realized that there was more to this anointing than I can ever comprehend, and yes, it is still well with my soul. I recall one Saturday afternoon I was feeling heartbroken, and I could not understand why; I said, "God, how much longer do I have to bear this pain in my heart? When will this be over?" And He replied, "The hearts that I am placing in your hands I don't want you to ever take them for granted; My grace is sufficient." Again, I rested because He ministered to my spirit, and I understood that my calling required heartbreak, so not only did I rest, I trusted Him that He would not give me more than I can bear.

"And they overcame him by the blood of the lamb, and by the word of their testimony; and they loved not their lives unto death" (Revelation 12:11, KJV).

There are days when my mind would take me back to my past, to where the enemy bruised my heel; the enemy would often remind me of where I was coming from. I would oftentimes think of the mat I slept on, and how lonely and afraid I was sleeping on the floor. I remember I would cry for my mother to save me, and I couldn't understand why I was there or why I was going through this. I often reflect on how I felt growing up in Jamaica; I always had a heaviness on my chest; it was like an elephant was just sitting there. But I was determined to get out of there. I oftentimes would fantasize about living in America; I knew if I got the opportunity to get here, I would be okay. I say this to say that your dreams will come true if you want it bad enough, God will bless it and make it your reality. I never knew that I would be sitting here, writing this book, but what God has done in my life, I am willing to set my pride aside and trust Him with my integrity so that my testimony can change or even bring one person to Christ. And that is my desire for this book: to heal the brokenhearted, open the eyes of the blind, and set the captives free from the bondage of the enemy.

In November 2019, while I was in worship, God gave me a vision. Every morning at 4:30 a.m., that was when I would have my devotion and prayer time with the Lord before work. But on this one particular morning, after I finished praying, God took me into the heavens.

THIS IS MY EXODUS

I was surrounded by the enemy and his fallen angels, they were far away from me, but I knew who they were, I was in the middle of that circle, but I was surrounded by five angels. I was kneeling, and my head was bowed down to the floor. I was in full white, and I was glowing, and then a hand descended from heaven, and oil began to flow from the hand unto my head. And the voice began to say, "Thou preparest a table before me in the presence of mine enemies: thou anointest my head with oil; my cup runneth over." I knew it was God, and even as He was repeating that well-known Psalm, the Holy Spirit was revealing to me that the enemy in the psalm was not people; oftentimes, we hear this particular scripture, we tend to think that the enemy is anyone that has done us wrong, but that is not true; the enemy in the scripture is the devil. After He was done anointing my head, the Lord gave me a message about humility, and He informed me to teach that message on breakfast with the Lord that same morning.

Every morning I would be on the phone at 7 a.m. with breakfast with the Lord; it's a prayer line that I was introduced to by my spiritual sister. On this line, saints gather together and do Bible study and encourage each other. Now on this line, we have pastors, evangelists, and prophets, pretty much most of the people on the line have twenty to thirty years of serving the Lord, and now God wants me to deliver a message that He gave me on humility. I was extremely nervous, but I had to be obedient to God; therefore, I delivered the message. It was amazing after I was through, and by the way, I spoke for about forty-five minutes, I took up all of the master speaker time, but she was graceful about it. Anyway, after I was done, to my surprise, everyone on the phone line was encouraged by my message and amazed how God was able to explain to me so clearly what humility means. After we hung up the phone, one of the evangelists called me and invited me to speak at her Overcomers Conference in Savannah, Georgia. This was a conference that she has every year, and I was invited to give my testimony and how amazing is our God; that is why it pays to be obedient to God.

"Having confidence in thy obedience I wrote unto thee, knowing that thou wilt also do more than I say" (Philemon 1:21, KJV).

I was excited for the opportunity to speak at the conference; I was also amazed at how God was using me and knowing that the same morning He anointed me and gave the message to teach. I was invited to speak at a conference. On November 8, 2019, the organization sent me the information that was formally inviting me to speak at their conference; the theme for the conference was "A Devine Exchange," and the scripture came from Zephaniah 3:19-20. While I was reading the scripture, I felt a familiarity with it, it was like I read it before, or God had given it to me in a dream.

As soon as I got home from work, I opened my Bible to the scripture, and to my amazement, I highlighted that passage in my Bible and dated it 05/27/2018. God gave me that scripture, and on that same day, He gave me a dream. I called the evangelist that was organizing the event, and I told her that God had given me that scripture on that particular day, and she said to me that God had given her that scripture around that same time, and she gave it to her pastor for such a time as this. I was in shock when those words left her mouth because everything she said to me was everything God gave to me in a dream, so right there and then, I knew that every promise that was in that scripture was a confirmed word from God, and I was to be in expectation of those promises.

> Behold, at that time I will undo all that afflict thee: and I will save her that halteth, and gather her that was driven out; and I will get them praise and fame in every land where they have been put to shame. At that time will I bring you again, even in the time that I gather you: for I will make you a name and a praise among all people of the earth, when I turn back your captivity before your eyes, saith the LORD.
>
> Zephaniah 3:19-20 (KJV)

As the time drew close for me to attend the conference, I began to get nervous because God was telling me that I had to speak on everything that I have been through, and not only that, He wanted me to bring a mat to demonstrate where the enemy bruised my heel. I was obedient, and I bought a brown mat, packed up my car, and drove to Savannah, Georgia, to deliver my testimony. On my way there, I was very afraid. The enemy was talking to me all the way there. He whispered, "Why are you going there to tell strangers about your shameful life? Are you really going there to tell church folk that you had abortions? You're going to disclose that you have been molested by different men and that your parents abandoned you." I began to feel ashamed and disgusted with myself, I was becoming weary and doubtful, so I turned to God and began to express my concerns and tell Him how I was feeling. I remembered after I was done expressing myself to Him, He simply said to me in a still small voice, "You can trust me with your integrity." I felt encouraged after that, but I was still nervous.

The conference lasted for three days, and I was scheduled to speak on the second night. I was still feeling fearful, but I did not want to be disobedient to God, so I was going to go through with it regardless of how I felt. The first speaker spoke on getting up; he preached on Jesus healing Peter's mother-in-law. The scripture is found in Luke 4:38-40. After Jesus spoke to her fever, He told her to get up. She had faith in Jesus's command, and because she had faith in His word, she got up and was made whole. It was a very good sermon because in accordance to me bringing the mat, God was also giving me a message about the man at the pool at Bethesda that was lying there for thirty-eight years, and it wasn't until Jesus asked him if he wanted to be made well and that he should pick up his mat and walk was when he got determined in his spirit and in his mind that he was tired of being lame and bound by the enemy. It was when he made up his mind to receive what Jesus was offering by faith that was when he was made whole.

"Jesus said to him, 'Rise, take up your bed and walk.' And immediately the man was made well, took up his bed, and walked" (John 5:8-9, NKJV).

I remember going to bed encouraged that night, and the next day I was ready to give my testimony. They introduced me, and I went up with my mat in my hand, and I gave my testimony; it was received well because after I was done speaking, the pastor that came to speak was unable to preach because my testimony hit home for her as well. She is also a prophetess, and she called me up in front of the entire church and prophesied to me. She told me that my book is going to be prophetic release, God was going to give me the tongue of the ready writer, but what was amazing she spoke about the book of Hebrews; she said that in the book of Hebrews, there is a rest that God gives to His people, and because I am going to dominate, I will receive this rest. She also prophesied 1 Corinthians 2:9. But the reason I was amazed when she mentioned the book of Hebrews was that a few months earlier, I was on a twenty-one-day Daniel fast, and during that fast, the Lord spoke to me and said that after I was done with the twenty-one-day fast, I should enter into a five-day absolute fast and during this fast, I should read the book of Hebrews. I obeyed, and I read the book of Hebrews, but to be honest, I did not get a connection or any revelation as to why God wanted me to read the book of Hebrews, but when the pastor mentioned it while prophesying to me, I knew I had to go back and read the book of Hebrews.

The conference was amazing; God did a mighty work that weekend, and I left my mat on the altar that night never to pick it up again because that was where the enemy bruised my heel, and that night I decided to accept what Jesus has for me—which is life, and it comes with abundance. Before I left on Sunday, I was surprised to see how many women came up to me, thanking me for my testimony. One woman said to me that she was sixty years old and she has not forgiven her mother because of what her mother had done to her; another woman came up to me and told me that she was raped as a child and has never spoken about it, this secret that has kept her bound for years and has even destroyed her marriage and because she had heard my testimony, she's willing now to confront her issues and work on them. Even the pastor had some confessions of her own; she, too, confessed about having an abortion. I left that conference empowered and faith-filled. God is truly the potter, and I am His clay; mold me, Lord, have Your way in my life.

I went back and read the book of Hebrews, but this time I read it with intent, and from then, I knew why God wanted me to read the book. The book of Hebrews matures us as Christians. To surmise the book, I would say this book teaches us that we have a high priest Jesus that came to die for our sins that we can go before God, our true Father, for help in times of struggle. This book also teaches us that we should rest in the Lord and in His promises because if you have unbelief, you can never enter God's rest. The book also made clear that Jesus came lower than the angels; He did not have any special powers, every miracle that He performed He did them by faith, and that is why the book of Hebrews tells us that without faith, it is impossible to please God. Also, while I was reading the book of Hebrews, God revealed to me that in Genesis, He rested on the seventh day; this meant that God was confident about what He has spoken over the earth. Whatever God has spoken must come to pass. Ultimately, the book of Hebrews or

I must say what God wanted me to know is that in order for me to enter into His rest, I have to have faith in Him because where He is taking me, I am going to need faith, so I must be determined in my mind and in my spirit that I will rest and trust that whatever He tells me, it is so and so it is.

"But without faith it is impossible to please him: for he that cometh to God must believe that he is, and that he is a rewarder of them that diligently seek him" (Hebrews 11:6, KJV).

The Bible tells us in Proverbs 13:12 that hope, deferred, makes the heart sick; sometimes, I wonder if we should even hope at all. How do we rest in God when what He has promised seems as if it will never come to pass? When my fiancé walked out on us, I heard a still small voice say to me, "It is not about you, it is about him, he needs to go, but I am going to let him return the man you want him to be." I question myself with this a lot because what I am seeing does not match up to what God has said, and for the first time in my life, I am struggling with my faith. But God is so patient and kind, He will always meet you where you're at spiritually, and as long as you are honest with him and open to receive His teachings, He will get you to where you need to be in whatever area of your life you are lacking faith. He will not bring what He has promised to pass just yet, but He will work in mysterious ways to build your faith and your confidence in Him, but most importantly, He will enlighten your eyes of understanding, and He will take you from faith to faith and glory to glory because we walk by faith and not by sight. "For we walk by faith, not by sight" (2 Corinthians 5:7, KJV).

As I mentioned earlier, God will work miracles and answer prayers right before your eyes so that whatever He has promised you will come to pass in your life, you see faith is what manifests the promise. I started working at a company back in September 2019, and I met a woman who confided in me that she was unable to have children, so I told her that I would pray for her and believe God for a miracle. I started praying for her, and God began to reveal to me what was wrong with her and why she couldn't conceive. You see, the enemy was wrapped around her fallopian tubes, but God was ready to reveal to us what we needed to do to bring this promise from the spiritual realm into the earthly realm. The first instruction the Holy Spirit gave me was to tell her to buy something for her baby and that she should read 1 Samuel chapter 2, Hannah's prayer, and declare it every day over her life. She was obedient to everything that God instructed her to do, but most importantly, she believed in God. In January 2020, she became pregnant. When she went to the doctor, they told her that she was twelve weeks pregnant; we began to trace back when this miracle took place. She conceived in November, and two weeks before her conception, that was when she bought the clothes and started declaring Hannah's prayer over her life.

"If ye be willing and obedient, ye shall eat the good of the land" (Isaiah 1:19, KJV). As I continue to embark on this journey with God, I began to see His heart for us and how much He loves us. Even though I am still being taught by the Holy Spirit, I can finally say I am beginning to see my way clear. I am beginning to walk more and more in the spirit of God, I see myself becoming more like His word, and I am now believing in Him and in His word. But I must admit there are days and moments when I find myself looking back, looking back at who I was, but mostly at what I have been through. The strangest thing is that I can see it, but I can't feel it, I often wonder why I do look back there, what I am looking for, and then it dawned on me; I am in a new place in my life, and I feel uncomfortable, I am happy but uncomfortable. Who knew that I would be looking back at my pain for comfort, or is it familiarity? I mean, in retrospect, I am kin to it and whatever you're kin to you, tend to want to hold on to.

The Father, the Son, and the Holy Ghost

I have learned that my trust is not in my obedience because God knows that I am going to fail; that is the reason He tells us in 2 Timothy 2:13 (KJV), "If we believe not, yet he abideth faithful: he cannot deny himself." That scripture gives me hope because there are days when I am struggling with my faith, but to know that He cannot deny Himself of remaining faithful to me even when I am faithless gives me peace in my soul. This scripture in 2 Timothy also holds weight for the scripture in Hebrews 11:6 (KJV) that states, "But without faith it is impossible to please him: for he that cometh to God must believe that he is, and that he is a rewarder of them that diligently seek him." If we as believers should be completely honest with ourselves, we can honestly say that there are moments when our faith or even our trust in God is completely low. As I reflected on that scripture in Hebrews, I felt like a failure because my faith was wavering, so automatically, I thought that I wasn't pleasing God.

The Holy Spirit is always there to minister to us, so as the enemy was condemning me, the teacher began to teach, he ministered to me by letting me know that God has given us all a measure of faith saved or unsaved, and that is the faith God is connected too. Not that God does not honor our faithfulness, but how many times you have kept the faith for something, and it never came to pass or trusted God wholeheartedly for something that you really wanted, and it never happens, this does not mean that your faith wasn't enough, it simply meant that God has something better and that something better is connected to that measure of faith. What I am trying to say is this God, our Father, delights in giving us the best. Luke 12:32 gives us a firm affirmation from God "Do not fear, little flock, for it is your Father's good pleasure to give you the kingdom" (Luke 12:32, NKJV).

Everything has an expiration date; your troubles will not last forever, and believe it or not, your joy too, but the one thing that remains constant is the word of the Lord. I know my season of grief is almost over, so while I am waiting for my season of joy, I prepare, and by preparing, I look at the season I am in now and work on the things that didn't work for me before I came into my season of grief. Therefore, if I am entering into a season of joy, I cannot bring anything from my season of grief, for example, unforgiveness, bitterness, sadness, and most importantly, the blame game; I love to point fingers, so that is the reason it is most important to me. So ask yourself what season of your life are you in now; even if it's a joyous season, you still have to prepare for your next season because it is coming, and most importantly, never prepare for your next season without the one who holds the blueprint to your life because that is the only way you will be able to withstand or prepare for your next season without fail.

Now that the work for this season is hopefully over, I reflect on how far I have come; I cannot believe that I have a Master's degree and a soon-to-be-published book. I never thought this would be my life; I never thought that I could accomplish this task that God has set before me, especially in the state I was in. The Holy Spirit is always revealing, so as I am typing, He gently whispered obedience is better than sacrifice; He began to remind me of stories in the Bible that show us that it was through obedience many victories have been won. It was through obedience the man at the pool of Bethesda was healed; it was through obedience David was able to recover all, and I could go on and on. God loves when we are obedient to His command even when our faith wavers, and as usual, He always reveals Himself through His word, "Walk in obedience to all that the Lord your God has commanded you, so that you may live and prosper and prolong your days in the land you will possess" (Deuteronomy 5:33, NIV).

Now that I have cleared the coffin and autopsied every hidden demon, I was ready for that which God has promised, that is, the restoration of my family. I was ready to be the wife God has prepared and called me to be, and I was a good mother, so here I am, Lord, but the days turn into weeks and the weeks turn into months, and of course, I became weary. As I wait patiently in faith and constant praise, God was silent; nothing was moving, it was as if I stepped back into purgatory, but I have grown so much in my God. I knew that He hadn't forsaken me; He was just testing me. Often, we believe that God's testing is in what we do to ourselves, meaning if we are weary and faithless, we fail, but that's not true. You see, He tells us that even when we are faithless, He is faithful because He cannot deny who He is, so where does this test come from? I remember it was a Sunday afternoon, and I had just finished watching my favorite Bishop preach, Bishop T. D. Jakes, and he preached on Luke 18:1-8, and the title of his sermon was "Bother me." Even though I had my own church that I was attending, God had given me a dream, and in that dream, He told me that during this time of preparation, I should glean from the bishop.

I am ashamed to say that I never knew about Bishop T. D. Jakes until God spoke to me in a dream and told me that it was through the bishop He would confirm His teachings in regards to my future. Therefore, I became an E-church member. Anyway, while I was on this journey of healing my soul, I was also on assignment; God had placed a few persons in my life that I was responsible for interceding in prayer for them, and guess what? They were all married. They were either having marital problems, struggling with sickness, or experiencing infertility; go figure because here I am trying to restore myself and waiting for my promise, and here comes God giving me assignments. But I enjoyed getting up early every morning, praying for those who He had placed in my hands, and let me tell you, it was a pleasure because He would use me to keep them faithful and encouraged.

The test, as I mentioned earlier, I was feeling drained and low in faith, and one of the persons I was interceding for called me. She was in the hospital because she was battling kidney disease for quite some time, and she was also battling with infertility. I have known her since childhood; we lived in the same neighborhood and attended the same church, but we weren't close, but I knew her. Anyway, it was in 2019 I was reading my Bible, and I was in the book of Genesis, and I came upon the scripture Genesis 30:22 (KJV), "And God remembered Rachel, and God hearkened to her, and opened her womb." I went to work the next morning, and the Holy Spirit would not leave me alone; with that scripture, I tried claiming it for myself, but it didn't feel right. I began going through my phone, and when I saw her name, I knew it was for her. I didn't know anything about her personal life at this point; the only thing I knew about her was that she was married.

I remembered that I sent her a message saying, "I hope this is something that you need today! I was reading my Bible last night, and when I got to Genesis 30:22, the Holy Spirit quickened my spirit! God remembers you." She replied by saying, "I am going to break down at work...I am struggling with believing that God remembers me where children are concerned. I have been doing tests upon tests, speaking the word, declaring...but I am struggling." I knew from then on she was to be added to my prayer list. Anyway, she developed kidney issues, and she was in the hospital, and she called me that Sunday for a little encouragement. I saw her calling, and for some reason, I didn't hesitate to answer. First, let me just say when I am in a mood, I do not speak to anyone, but I knew she needed me, so I pulled myself together, and we prayed, and I encouraged her in the Lord, and believe me, I came off the phone encouraged. And that was my test, am I going to be faithful to the hearts, He is placing in my hands even when my faith is failing, it was then I understood that it wasn't in my strength that I would be used by God, but it would be in His.

The Holy Spirit, my "teacher," as I continue on this mind-blowing journey with God, His revelations or His teachings drew me closer to who I am and who He is; in fact, His teachings draw me closer to Jesus Christ, and He gives me a deeper understanding of why He died for us.

> But the Comforter, which is the Holy Ghost, whom the Father will send in my name, he shall teach you all things, and bring all things to your remembrance, whatsoever I have said unto you.
>
> John 14:26 (KJV)

I have heard of God, the Father, and the Holy Ghost, but to be honest, I had no true understanding of what they all meant and how I was to communicate with them or how they were to communicate to me until I was reading this verse in the book of John. My spirit immediately leaped when Jesus Christ told His disciples that God is sending the Holy Spirit in Jesus's name to be our Comforter. Wow! Immediately, God began to reveal to me that the one who lives inside of me is Jesus Christ, and He intercedes for us; He told me that whenever Jesus came to Him on my behalf, He does not question nor does He ponder on the request because He believes in the one who He has sent. I began to realize that my only job is to believe in the one that He has sent, who is our Comforter, the Holy Spirit that was sent in the name of Jesus Christ; not only does He comforts us, but He reveals and shows us things to come.

Who Am I?

"But the fruit of the Spirit is love, joy, peace, long-suffering, gentleness, goodness, faith, Meekness, temperance: against such there is no law" Galatians 5:22-23 (KJV).

"Who are you?" God softly whispered in my ear, and as I was about to say the things I know, He wanted to hear my conscience wouldn't allow me to utter such deception. I wasn't going to lie to my God because He and I have come too far on this journey for me to be deceptive, and furthermore, whenever God asks a question, He already knows the answer, and most importantly, I wanted the revelation that He was about to give. He allowed me to ponder on this question for two days, and it was hard for me because I never stopped to think about who I am. I was so busy trying to create myself in my own image because I didn't want to fail. I didn't want to fail, not for my sake but for the bystanders, who were eagerly awaiting my downfall.

Up to this point in my life, everything that I have accomplished was based on the fact that no one expected me to be where I am today, but it was their lowly expectations that drove me to become successful. A diamond doesn't become a beautiful diamond without applying heat and pressure, so maybe some of us require lowly expectations to achieve. But this was still unsettling to me because in order for me to achieve, I have to be surrounded by negativity. Is that who I am, someone who thrives on other people's devious assumptions on the outcome of my life. That's just it; God wanted to show me that I was fueled by the ignorance of others, who were also struggling with their own identity to determine mine, so again, He asks, "Who are you?"

As I reflect on 2017, when my fiancé left my children and me, and how devastated I was, I am now beginning to understand the question. I blamed God for taking away my family, but He didn't; I still had myself and my two beautiful children, but because my identity was again wrapped up in the perspective of someone else's opinion about me when he left, he also took me that got lost in him. Isn't it funny how we unintentionally hide from ourselves? For me, it was my fiancé. I was so caught up in him and making him happy that I forgot about him. But did I really forget about me, or was I using him to fix the little girl that was lost within me? One of the reasons I gravitated to my fiancé was because we had familiar pain. Isn't it funny how spirits attract spirit? Out of all the men I have ever been with, I chose to give him my heart because my little broken girl was attracted to his little broken boy, and it was easier to fix me through him. Even though I thought that I was fixing him, I was actually punishing myself for him because, in reality, I hated who I was or the things that had happened to me. So, I hid in him because he, too, had the characteristics of my little broken girl.

Genesis 1:27 tells us that God created man in His own image and in the image of God; He created them. I know somewhere in those words is who I am; I have read this passage many times as a child, and as an adult, I have even quoted this passage for affirmation, but to be honest, I never recognized that those two sentences hold my true identity. Therefore, to find out who I am, I must first find out who He is. I was determined to find this other missing piece to my Exodus, and I also knew I was approaching the end of my book, so I began to quote scriptures of who He says I am, like "I am the head and not the tail," "I am above and not beneath." You know scriptures that breathe life into our souls when the enemy casts doubt on our integrity. But my spirit was still dormant, and besides, I have now developed a relationship with God to know when He speaks to my spirit.

I then researched who does God says He is, and a few of His Judaism names came up in my search, and they were: El Roi, El Elyon, Jehovah Jireh, just to name a few. I was so excited when I came across these names because for the past two years. I would participate in a twenty-one-day fast, and in 2019, the theme for that year was the names of God. So, I was sure that this was the place I would find out who God is and my identity. I read each of those names and their meanings, desperately trying to see how I was connected to those names through Him, but again there was no revelation because I realized that even though that's who He is, those names were given to Him. For example, Jehovah Jireh was given to Him by Abraham, which means the Lord is my provider, and El Roi was given to Him by Hagar, which means the God who sees. So, these names had some sentimental attachments to God and the ones who gave them to Him, so, therefore, it would be unfitting for me to try and find my identity in someone else's inauguration of God.

God is so patient with us, and if you seek Him, you will find Him, and He is definitely a rewarder of those who diligently seek Him. Now at the end of myself feeling cast down but not destroyed, my Father then steps in to teach. He then led me to the book of Galatians. Galatians 5:22-23 (KJV), "But the fruit of the Spirit is love, joy, peace, longsuffering, gentleness, goodness, faith, Meekness, temperance: against such there is no law." Immediately, my spirit rejoiced because I knew I was about to be rewarded; e then took me back to Genesis1:1-2:

> In the beginning God created the heaven and the earth. And the earth was without form, and void; and darkness was upon the face of the deep. And the Spirit of God moved upon the face of the waters.
>
> Genesis1:1-2 (KJV)

Genesis is where God tells us that He is a Spirit, and Galatians is where God tells us that we are His fruit. Remember, in Genesis 1:27, He tells us that we are made in His own image and in the image of God, He created us. However, in verse 28 of that same chapter, God blesses us and tells us that we should be fruitful and multiply, and in doing so, it simply means that our offsprings or our children are seen as fruits in the eyes of God. Therefore, in Galatians, where it tells us what the fruit of the Spirit is, it translates as the children of God—love, joy, peace, longsuffering, gentleness, goodness, faith, meekness, and temperance—are who we are. So with confidence and boldness, I can say I know who I am; I am the *fruit* of the *Spirit*.

Basking in this heavenly revelation from my Father, I recognized that I was gaining insight on the meaning of 2 Corinthians 10:4 (KJV): "For the weapons of our warfare are not carnal, but mighty through God to the pulling down of strong holds." I then ask the question, "What are my strongholds? What is it that I am laying bare before the enemy that he is using against me to not bear the fruits that are required by God? The word carnal relates to physicality, so I am associating my fruit with my feelings, not realizing that God is a Spirit so, therefore, the fruits I bear must firstly be established in the spirit, so it's safe to say that my biggest stronghold is relying on my feelings or my emotions to determine the fruits that I bare.

The Holy Spirit once revealed to me that my feelings or emotions do not depict my beliefs. God does not judge me based on the inconsistency of my feelings but the consistency of my heart, which is, by the way, my soul, where my mind also dwells. Consequently, before producing those fruits, I must first be connected to the spirit, and by doing so, I have to seek Him first, not His promises, but the one who promised. I don't know about other Christians and how they fell in love with God, but I couldn't do it on my own or in my own strength. I was tired of saying I love you, Lord, because the pastor told me to or because He woke me up and put a roof over my head and food on the table. Don't get me wrong, those are wonderful things to love God for, but I wanted to be in love with Him; I wanted to say, "I love you, Lord" with no reservations, not for what He's done, but for who He is.

> Love is patient and kind. Love is not jealous or boastful or proud or rude. It does not demand its own way. It is not irritable, and it keeps no record of being wronged. It does not rejoice about injustice but rejoices whenever the truth wins out. Love never gives up, never loses faith, is always hopeful, and endures through every circumstance.
>
> 1 Corinthians 13:4-7 (NLT)

This is the love that binds me to the spirit of God; the Bible also tells us that love covers a multitude of sin; so, therefore, if I practice this kind of love, then when offenses come, and they will because Jesus tells us this in Luke 17, I am not reluctant to forgive. This is where I become a doer of the word, now that I have heard it, I must now receive it into my heart and soul, and once the circumcision has taken place, which it has then bearing my fruits....let me say that again: bearing *my fruits!* I will forever be connected to my Lord and Savior, Jesus Christ.

"Amazing grace—how sweet the sound that saved a wretch like me..." As I reflect on my journey and how the grace of God led me to salvation, overwhelming tears of gratitude rolled down my cheeks as I gentle drifted into the presence of God, giving thanks to those unrecognized moments when He looked beyond my faults and saw my needs. The story of Rahab, the prostitute, came to me and how God heard her cry for deliverance and He saved her in spite of her sins and David, who lusted, fornicated, lied, and killed, yet God saw his heart and loved him anyway. And of course, those moments when I could've died having an abortion or being locked up in prison when I trafficked drugs, but the unmerited, undeserved favor of God snatched me up before the enemy could have his way, and now, here, I am drenched in the blood of the lamb and empowered by the word of my testimony.

As I rejoiced in yet another victory, the Holy Spirit gently whispered, "Now that you have accepted the grace of God for your own indiscretions, are you now willing to give that same grace to your offenders?" I immediately understood what the Holy Spirit was implying; you see, the grace isn't for my past offenders; it is for the ones to come. It is for the best friend who is about to point me out to my accusers, the family member who is, of course, going to remind me of who I was, and the enemy in me that occasionally screams, "You are not good enough." Again He whispered, "Will your offenders obtain the same grace you were given?" As I was about to answer, I recognize that it wasn't a question; it was an expectation and preparation for my ordered steps.

The faithfulness of God is one I now hold on to; you see, God isn't faithful because I go to church, pay my tithe, or because I do good things. God is faithful because that's who He is; that's His nature. Second Timothy 2:13 (NKJV) tells us, "If we are faithless, He remains faithful; He cannot deny Himself." My God! What love! Even when I am doubting in His faithfulness towards me, He is still for me; who wouldn't serve a God such as this. The grace of God should not be taken carelessly; I deliberately chose to use the word "carelessly" because how can we as believers so nonchalantly take this gift for granted. Titus 2:11 (NLT) tells us, "For the grace of God has been revealed, bringing salvation to all people." As believers, it was the grace of God that got us our salvation so that we may enter not only into heaven, but it has kept us through many dangers, toils, and sneers. Again, I look back, and I think you should too. If it wasn't for His grace and mercy, where would we be?

"For by grace are ye saved through faith; and that not of yourselves: it is the gift of God" (Ephesians 2:8, KJV).

For the Battle Is Not Yours

Looking back on my life, I realized that I was fighting a battle I didn't choose. As I reminisced on the little girl who desperately fought to survive in a conundrum, she was born into my heart ached for her. How did I survive those moments of despair, shame, and loneliness? What or who kept me in the fight? Because there were many days, I was sure it was my last round, but here I am, still fighting. The biggest fight for me was being abandoned by parents; people treated me with contempt because I was abandoned as if it was my fault like this was something I chose, like I told my parents to toss me away like trash. I've had adults who literally told me that it was my fault that my parents didn't want me and aunts who told my cousins that they shouldn't speak to me because I have the characteristics of my mother. I'm assuming that they meant I was no good.

And just like that, I was put in a fight that would ultimately define me as I stumbled through life.

I never gave in to their disparaging innuendos, although they were crippling moments when I thought about yielding to their concept of what my life should be, I never did. There was something in me that kept on pulling me towards a greater purpose; I knew this wasn't supposed to be my life; there was always an unsettling feeling that I was created for more. I've had some unexplainable miracles in my life; that was, undoubtedly, the hand of God, and those were the moments that sparked my curiosity to keep pushing because I was curious to see what was on the other side of this battle that I was reluctantly chosen to fight.

I have often heard, spoken, and sang these words: "For the battle is not yours, it's the Lord's" without understanding the sovereignty in its meaning, without realizing that God was telling me that He was responsible for this battle, I was in. He was the one who chose my parents; yes, God was the mastermind behind my pain and anguish. I know it sounds harsh, but it's the truth, He chose the path for me because if I had to choose, I would not have chosen these people to be my parents, and I am sure I am not alone when I say this. I am sure if some of us were given the opportunity to choose our parents, we would've chosen better. But not to be too judgmental on our parents' character, I am sure they, too, have their own stories, and I am sure they, too, wished they could've chosen their paths as well.

In order for me to truly accept the battle I was chosen for, I must first find the cause. Why would the God of love choose such a path for me, a helpless child, to endure such shame and pain? And then I thought about Jesus Christ, who so selfishly died on the cross for me when I was His enemy. Even though Jesus is the Son of God, He, too, was reluctantly chosen by God to carry out a mission that brought sorrow to His soul.

> Then saith he unto them, My soul is exceeding sorrowful, even unto death: tarry ye here, and watch with me. And he went a little farther, and fell on his face, and prayed, saying, O my Father, if it be possible, let this cup pass from me: nevertheless not as I will, but as thou wilt.
>
> Matthew 26:38-39 (KJV)

That is one of the most powerful scriptures I have ever read; this scripture shows that even the Son of God was apprehensive in accepting the battle He was chosen for; He exclaimed that His soul was exceeding sorrowful, meaning that His whole being was in turmoil, He was in pain, and to think that He was just in expectancy of what was to come, He wasn't even experiencing the reality of His faith, but just the thought of what is to come to His whole being was warped in anguish. And then He said the one thing that made the battle come into focus "nevertheless not as I will, but as thou wilt," and there it is the cause, the reason the battle chose me.

I was chosen because of His will and His purpose. Psalm 24:1 (KJV) distinctively tells us, "The earth is the LORD's, and the fulness thereof; the world, and they that dwell therein." Therefore, the battles we face it's not ours,' it's His, and oh, what a privilege and honor to bear these scars; you see, scars are not only reminders that we were once in a battle and we overcame, they are what we use to heal others like our Savior Jesus Christ consistently does for us. Isaiah 53: 5 (KJV): "But he was wounded for our transgressions, he was bruised for our iniquities: the chastisement of our peace was upon him; and with his stripes we are healed." I know to some it may seem as if I am comparing myself to Jesus, but Philippians 1:21 (KJV) tells us, "For to me to live is Christ, and to die is gain." Paul, an apostle of the gospel and the writer of many books in the Bible, including Philippians, was merely reminding us that we all are to live as Christ did, we should emulate His life knowing that we are victorious through any and all circumstances because even in death, we gain eternal life to one day be with Jesus Christ our King and Savior.

How privy am I to be personally handpicked by God to carry out His "mission"? He could've chosen anyone to bear these scars because, in the end, it is He who gets the glory, honor, and praise. And to think that the God of the universe, The Alpha and Omega, the beginning and the end chose me to bring Him glory in the earth, with a battle I was ashamed of and scars that the enemy tried to use and define me. But the battle was never mine, to begin with; so, victory was inevitable. Our God tells us in Romans 8:28 (KJV), "And we know that all things work together for good to them that love God, to them who are the called according to his purpose." Again, there it is, it was a calling, and because I am His sheep, I followed His voice to fulfill His purpose in His battle.

Complete Victory

How did I get here? Reflecting on my journey, my life's journey, that is, I shook my head in utter amazement and disbelief at how far I have come; I never thought that I would one day be a published author and, above all else, the miraculous, inspirational, unbreakable bond that I have developed with my Father in heaven. Looking back on the peculiar circumstances that I emerged from is a testament in itself and a revelation of Proverbs 20:24 (NKJV): "A man's steps are of the LORD; How then can a man understand his own way?" Amen to that! Now I must put aside my journey for a while and venture into the life of Ruth; some of us are familiar with her story in the Bible, which is, of course, found in the book of Ruth. Oftentimes when this sermon is preached, it's taken from a perspective of Ruth's loyalty to her mother-in-law, Naomi, and because of this loyalty, she ended up with a husband and great wealth. But the Holy Spirit wanted me to take

Ruth's story from a different approach and find out how Ruth got there.

As I began to read the book of Ruth, I realized that she was introduced to us as a Moabites; Moabites in the Bible, according to Judges 11:24, is a tribe of people who are known to worship an idol god, whom they call Chemosh, therefore, Ruth was an idol worshipper. If you are familiar with the story of Ruth, you know that she married a Judean named Mahlon, who was the son of Naomi. Let's backtrack a little for my readers that are not familiar with the story of Ruth. Naomi, Ruth's mother-in-law, was from Bethlehem. She and her husband and two sons fled to Moab because there was a famine in their land; hence, they had to find food in order to live, and that's how they ended up in Moab. I wanted to make a point about Ruth being an idol worshipper and her husband, Mahlon, being a Judean. You see, Judeans believe in only one God; so, therefore, the thought of worshipping idols was detestable to them. In fact, these are the descendants of Moses, or should I say the ten commandments, adamant believers; if you are not familiar with the ten commandments, you can find them in Exodus 20, the first commandment states: "You shall have no other gods before me." And the second, which is Exodus 20:4, says: "You must not make for yourself an idol of any kind or an image of anything in the heavens or on the earth or in the sea." Judeans were militant in their religion, so how did an idol worshipper and a man of godly principles get married?

As I delve further into the background of Ruth, I was curious to find out about her ancestors; I wanted to know about her descendants and why she was chosen by God to be an offspring of Jesus Christ. Oh, yes, Ruth, the idolatress, is in the bloodline of Jesus Christ. Both she and her husband, Boaz, started the family of King David, the David I speak of is the David that slew Goliath. This story can be found in 1 Samuel 17 for the readers who are not familiar with this story. Anyway, I went all the way back into the book of Genesis to Noahs' genealogy, and there I gained a little knowledge. Noah was Lots' uncle, the Lot I speak of is the story found in Genesis 19, but the verse most of us are familiar with is verse 26 when Lots' wife disobeyed the angel of God's command and looked back at Sodom and Gomorrah, a city that was being destroyed by God; and she turned into a pillar of salt, yes, that Lot. Anyway, Lot had two daughters, according to Genesis 19:30, and when he and his two daughters fled from the destruction of God, they ended up living in a cave.

According to Genesis 19:31-38, Lots' daughters decided to get their father drunk and sleep with him because, according to them, they wanted to preserve their father's lineage. The two nameless daughters' of Lot succeeded, and they both got pregnant by their father, the eldest daughter gave birth to a son, and she named him Moab, and the youngest also gave birth to a son, and his name was Ben-ammi. Therefore, I conclude that Ruth is the descendant of Lot, being that Lot's daughter, the son whose name is Moab, who went on to be the father of the Moabites. I then wondered to myself if Ruth knew her story and if that was what motivated her to marry a Judean and stay with her mother-in-law, Naomi, even though she knew Naomi had nothing to offer her.

> Return home, my daughters; I am too old to have another husband. Even if I thought there was still hope for me—even if I had a husband tonight and then gave birth to sons—would you wait until they grew up? Would you remain unmarried for them? No, my daughters. It is more bitter for me than for you, because the LORD's hand has turned against me!
>
> Ruth 1:12-13 (NIV)

Why did Orpah turn back? Ruth 1:15 (KJV): "And she said, Behold, thy sister in law is gone back unto her people, and unto her gods: return thou after thy sister in law." Wow! Orpah did not only return to her people, but she returned to her gods, meaning she went back to being an idolatress. Even though she married a Judean, unlike Ruth, Orpah wasn't fully convinced of her husband's God, or her motives outweighed her desires. The Holy Spirit revealed to me that true conversion or circumcision comes from the heart.

> A person is not a Jew who is one only outwardly, nor is circumcision merely outward and physical. No, a person is a Jew who is one inwardly; and circumcision is circumcision of the heart, by the Spirit, not by the written code. Such a person's praise is not from other people, but from God.
>
> Romans 3:28-29 (NIV)

The Holy Spirit began to reveal to me that; so it is amongst most believers, their motives towards the Lord outweigh their desire for Him. Most people baptize because they do not want to go to hell or they believe that the Lord is a genie in a bottle; they don't truly desire to know Him, to seek His face, and fear Him reverentially. Proverbs 9:10 (NIV) states: "The fear of the LORD is the beginning of wisdom, and knowledge of the Holy One is understanding," and how many believers lack understanding because they do not truly desire the Lord. Therefore, like Orpah, when the travesties of life rear it's ugly head, they quickly turn back to their sin because their hearts never truly believed, and with any storms in life, whether it be a marriage in trouble or a friendship being tested, the intensity of these storms will always produce the true motive of one's heart.

The things we desire are truly not our own; Ruth's steps were already ordained by God, as was Naomi's. The Holy Spirit revealed to me that Ruth was aware of her ancestors' immorality, and she desired to break that curse from her life; so, marrying a Judean was intentional for Ruth, and by doing so, she denounced her God Chemosh and accepted Judaism. God will always prepare you for your destination; Ruth had no idea that this conversion was her "passport" into a wealthy place. You see, the Judeans were not so accepting as the Moabites were; they were steadfast in their beliefs, so Ruth, going back to Bethlehem, would spark controversy, but because she had married Mahlon, a Judean, her authenticity would have already been established. Also, Naomi had no incline that she, too, would one day lose everything in Moab and would have to return to Bethlehem. You see, the famine was over in Bethlehem, and because Naomi lost her husband and sons, she decided to go back home to escape the memories of all she had lost. Naomi was bitter against God; she exclaimed, "The LORD's hand has turned against me" (Ruth 1:13, NIV).

I completely identify with Naomi's bitterness; I have also concluded some time or the other that the Lord's hand has turned against me, and there was absolutely no way for me to arise from these ashes. And I can also mirror Ruth's decision in choosing a different path from the one she was born into, and then, without warning here, comes adversity. Even though it was Naomi who lost the most, it was Ruth's determination I was most in tune with. I understood what it meant to desire a life different from the one you were given and then to watch it all crumble before your eyes and not have the ability to save it. Ruth was determined to live a different life that God had strategically placed in her heart; yes, she was loyal to Naomi, but Ruth had a burning desire for something she could not explain: a desire that made her make a declaration and commitment to a woman who considered herself as bitter.

> And Ruth said, Intreat me not to leave thee, or to return from following after thee: for whither thou goest, I will go; and where thou lodgest, I will lodge: thy people shall be my people, and thy God my God: Where thou diest, will I die, and there will I be buried: the LORD do so to me, and more also, if ought but death part thee and me.
>
> Ruth 1:16-17 (KJV)

Hope! That was the desire that burned so deeply within Ruth. In fact, I have now concluded that hope is what has kept me going for so long; that indescribable pull I have always felt was the hope of God that He has so graciously given to us. Psalm 62:5 (NIV) tells us, "Yes, my soul, find rest in God; my hope comes from him." If my hope comes from God, then everything that I hope for will ultimately come to pass in my life; therefore, my thoughts and my desires must align with the will of God. The Bible tells us that it is with the mind we serve the Lord, and by doing so, we must be cognizant of the things we think about. But I am not ignorant to the enemy's devices; you see, we have an enemy that sometimes assaults our minds, but Paul has given a strategy to overcome the enemy's devices.

> Finally, brethren, whatsoever things are true, whatsoever things are honest, whatsoever things are just, whatsoever things are pure, whatsoever things are lovely, whatsoever things are of good report; if there be any virtue, and if there be any praise, think on these things.
>
> Philippians 4:8 (KJV)

When the word of God abides within us, then the fiery darts of the enemy will not prevail. Second Timothy 2:15 (KJV) tells us: "Study to shew thyself approved unto God, a workman that needeth not to be ashamed, rightly dividing the word of truth." And we know that only the truth, which is the word of the Lord, makes us free.

Does the truth really make us free? It depends on the truth, I guess, because as I dove deeper into Ruth's life, her truth does not seem like freedom. How does knowing that you came from incest make you free? I would think this would make you bitter and resentful like Naomi was, and then it hit me, I mean the Holy Spirit revealed to me that oftentimes, the thing that stares us in the face that is known as opposition is who we are, a teacher nonetheless, because sometimes if we are not forcibly faced with our truths, we never become free. Therefore, knowing them and facing them literally is the path to true freedom. As I sit here writing this book, I am faced with my truth and my opposition, and I am wondering how do I become free? It's not like I have a Naomi or a field to glean in for my Boaz, so I ask myself, or should I say the Holy Spirit who reveals all things, "How do I become free?"

Our freedom is sometimes wrapped up in fear, fear of the unknown, fear of the outcome of our lives, and the most convenient one is the fear that plague the mind of the believer, and that is trusting God with that which we have placed in His hands or that which He has promised. First John 4:18 (KJV) states: "There is no fear in Love; but perfect love casteth out fear: because fear hath torment. He that feareth is not made perfect in love." The love that the scripture speaks of here is God Himself; you see, 1 John 4:8 (NIV) tells us: "Whoever does not love does not know God, because God is love." Therefore, 1 John 4:18 is telling us that there is no fear in God and because He is the perfect love, we should not be afraid. Job 3:25 (KJV): "For the thing which I greatly feared is come upon me, and that which I was afraid of is come unto me." I can definitely identify with Job here; I was so afraid to lose my family, and in fearing this, I went into agreement with the enemy, and because I was harboring the spirit of fear, I lost my family.

I really wanted to get a true revelation on how to rid fear when it rears its ugly head; so not being satisfied with the Holy Spirit's revelation, I dug deeper into the scriptures, I asked God to give me a deeper understanding of who He is, and then without fail, He answered. He led me to 1 Corinthians 13:4-8:

> Love is patient, love is kind. It does not envy, it does not boast, it is not proud. It does not dishonor others, it is not self-seeking, it is not easily angered, it keeps no record of wrongs. Love does not delight in evil but rejoices with the truth. It always protects, always trusts, always hopes, always perseveres. Love never fails...
>
> 1 Corinthians 13:4-8 (NIV)

This is who God is because He told us in 1 John 4:8 that He (God) is love; then, if we substitute the word love for God in 1 Corinthians 13:4-8, then 1 John 4:18 holds true. There is absolutely no fear in love (God) because He is perfect in all my fears. He has surely set us free!

As I close this chapter in my life and welcome the new beginning that awaits me, I give glory to God. This has truly been a remarkable journey I never thought I could have endured, let alone be set free on a level where my freedom has now become my mission. I say it has become my mission because not only have I experienced the counsel and wisdom of God, I have now embodied His spirit within me that I am now ready to impart upon others. I am now ready to love as He loves, I am now ready to give as He gives, and most importantly, I am ready to walk victoriously because greater is He that is in me than He that is in the world.

Epilogue

I made it! I made it! I made it!

When I think of the goodness of Jesus and all that He has done for me, my soul cries out *Hallelujah!* I am smiling from ear to ear as I write my *epilogue*...that statement alone in itself makes my heart rejoice in the Lord. As I nonchalantly glanced at what is behind me, I triumphantly but humbly rejoice, rejoicing because I won; I never succumbed to the enemies' lies; I fought for my freedom. I have gained integral confidence about myself that I never believed could be mine, I have tasted, and I have seen that the Lord is good; I no longer lead nor do live in *fear*. I am now living and leading from a place of *love!*

All my fruits are in alignment with the spirit of the Lord; I hear Him so clearly, now His spirit rests upon me every day, and most importantly, I am now His sheep because I know His voice. The Good Shepherd He is, to know that I was the one sheep that strayed away, and without hesitating, He came and rescued me. And like the prodigal son, He welcomed me in His arms, not making mention of the stench I carried, the stench of unrighteous living, but immediately He began clothing me in His righteousness and cleansed me from all unrighteousness.

You, too, can be made whole, I started out wanting what I thought was what I needed to be happy, and that was having a family, but what is a family if it is not built by the Lord? The Bible tells us in Psalm 127:1 (NIV): "Unless the LORD builds the house, the builders labor in vain. Unless the LORD watches over the city, the guards stand watch in vain." He has built my house with love, joy, peace, patience, gentleness, goodness, and faithfulness. Never stop fighting and never stop believing because if He did it for me, *God* will definitely do it for *you*!

"Being confident of this very thing, that he which hath begun a good work in you will perform it until the day of Jesus Christ" (Philippians 1:6, KJV).

About the Author

Makenee Makeda is a devoted Christian mother of two beautiful children and an author who was born on the beautiful Island of Jamaica and currently lives in Florida. She holds a master's degree in Healthcare Law from Nova Southeastern University. Writing has always been a passion for her; inspired by her own life's journey, she has decided to inspire others with her testimony. Having served on the prayer team and on the choir at her church, she considers herself a servant leader. She believes that her book will help heal the wounds of the oppressed and help them break free from the shackles of the injustice that were pressed upon them in their time of vulnerability and moments when darkness was all we knew. But God, who came and gave us life in abundance, has set her free from the enemy that bruised her heel.